Praise for the Dating Goddess

The *Adventures in Delicious Dating After 40* series of books is based on the blog Adventures in Delicious Dating After 40 at www.DatingGoddess.com. Here are comments from readers.

♥ "Adventures in Delicious Dating After 40 is a wonderful composite of both the mechanics of post-40 online dating and what the practice of honoring one's self actually looks like. How marvelous your writing is to read. I spent about 2 hours reading and was riveted the whole time." —Maggie Hanna

♥ "At last, a dating writer who addresses requirements. You are SO right on! I'm thrilled to have found you!" —Rachel Sarah, author, *Single Mom Seeking*

♥ "Powerfully heartfelt and honest writing. You are inspiring." —Kare Anderson, Emmy Award winning writer

"I just love your writing. It is very fresh and gives the reader something to think about." —Kelly Lantz, President & Manager, 55-Alive.com

"Dating Goddess, you are like a, a, a, well, a goddess to me. You've helped guide me successfully through my re-entry into the dating world after 14 years. I'm an eager student and fast study, and do get myself into situations that others don't know how to deal with — such as 3 dates in one day — so thankfully you are there! You're the greatest, thanks for all you do for us!" —Jae G.

"Thanks for a wonderful blog. You're doing a great job of saying what's in my mind. There's rarely a day I miss when it comes to checking in on your wisdom." —Paulette Ensign

"I love Adventures in Delicious Dating After 40. I really do like your honest and authentic voice — it's refreshing." —Wendy S.

"Adventures in Delicious Dating After 40 is really fun to read. Thanks for sharing your thoughts and letting us divorced single women know that we are not alone. There's a lot here that I identify with, although I'm not as brave as you are about dating lots of guys. So far. Love your blog — the first blog I've ever read consistently." —Elizabeth

Ironing Out Dating Wrinkles

Work Through Challenges Without Getting Steamed

by **Dating Goddess**

Ironing Out Dating Wrinkles: Work Through Challenges Without Getting Steamed

Cover design by Dave Innis, www.innisanimation.com

Book design by JustYourType.biz

Printed in the United States of America.

ISBN   Print: 978-1-930039-90-2

eBook: 978-1-930039-23-0

How to order:

The *Adventures in Delicious Daing After 40* books may be ordered directly from www.DatingGoddess.com.

Quantity discounts are also available. Visit us online for updates and additional articles.

*The Adventures in Delicious
Dating After 40 books are ded-
icated to my ex-husband since
he unexpectedly released me to
explore the untethered life of a
single woman. I then had the
freedom for the experiences,
lessons and insights shared in
these pages.*

Books by Dating Goddess

♥ Date or Wait: Are You Ready for Mr. Great?

♥ Assessing Your Assets: Why You're A Great Catch

♥ In Search of King Charming: Who Do I Want to Share My Throne?

♥ Embracing Midlife Men: Insights Into Curious Behaviors

♥ Dipping Your Toe in the Dating Pool: Dive In Without Belly Flopping

♥ Winning at the Online Dating Game: Stack the Deck in Your Favor

♥ Check Him Out Before Going Out: Avoiding Dud Dates

♥ First-Rate First Dates: Increasing the Chances of a Second Date

♥ Real Deal or Faux Beau: Should You Keep Seeing Him?

♥ Multidating Responsibly: Play the Field Without Being A Player

♥ Moving On Gracefully: Break Up Without Heartache

♥ From Fear to Frolic: Get Naked Without Getting Embarrassed

♥ Ironing Out Dating Wrinkles: Work Through Challenges Without Getting Steamed

Contents

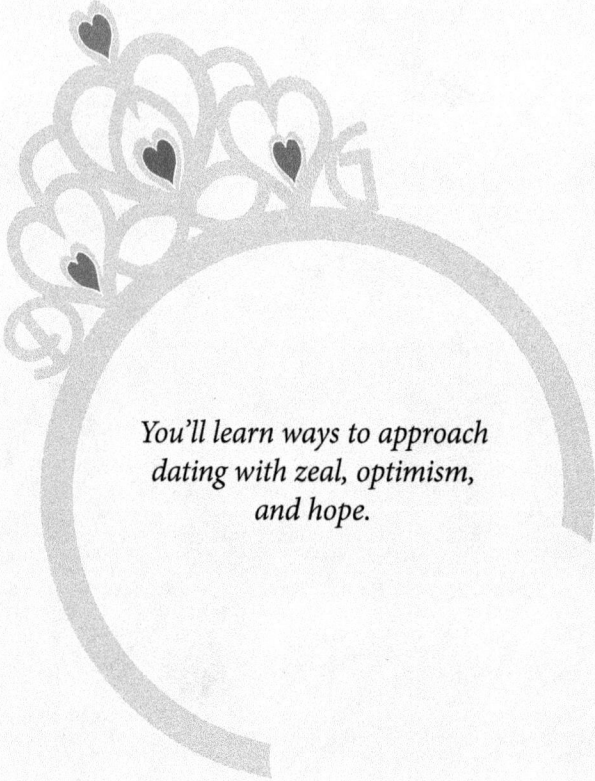

You'll learn ways to approach dating with zeal, optimism, and hope.

Introduction

This book is designed for anyone who is interested in stories, advice, and lessons from the midlife dating front. If you are over 40 and haven't dated in a while — or even if you have — you'll learn ways to approach dating with zeal, optimism, and hope. Even if you've had more than your share of negative experiences, I'll share how to glean lessons from those adventures, rather than just declaring that "all men are jerks" or "men are just looking for sex."

While most of the perspective is from a woman to women, men's comments, experiences, and lessons have been integrated as appropriate.

This book began as daily entries into my blog, Adventures in Delicious Dating After 40, which has been featured in the *Wall Street Journal* as well as on radio and TV. I wrote about my epiphanies from my and my friends' dating life. The best postings were culled to make this and subsequent books.

This book focuses on how to work through the inevitable hiccups that happen when you are getting to know each other. If you can both deal with challenges, the bond deepens and you find yourself smitten.

This book consists of three types of perspectives:

💜 **Lessons:** These are specific experiences I thought would be useful to you. A few lines from my experience illustrate the points.

💜 **Insights:** These usually start with an experience I've encountered, then the insights that experience spawned. It is usually comprised of around half story and half insight.

💜 **Stories:** These are examples of situations I've experienced — or was currently experiencing when I wrote that piece — that I thought would be entertaining. Or I thought the story would help you see what kind of things happen in the midlife dating world so you'd know what has happened to others.

Because these writings were real time, as they occured, they are often set in the present tense. But they are not chronological. So a reference to "my current beau" may now be many sweethearts ago. I hope this isn't confusing.

I'd love ot hear your stories and questions. Please email them to me at Goddess@DatingGoddess.com. They may make it into the blog or my next book!

Who is the Dating Goddess?

I am a middle-aged, white, professional woman. My husband of nearly 20 years left me in April 2003 when I was 47, 11 days shy of 48. After giving my heart time to heal from the surprise divorce sprung by the man I thought was my soulmate, I started dating 18 months later. Generally, I have had a great time meeting interesting men, some of whom became romantic beaus, some became treasured friends, and some I never heard from again.

> *I am not a well-preserved, gorgeous, marathon-running middle-aged women*

In the beginning, I had dates with single male colleagues, but I quickly found Internet dating was the way to explore the most "inventory" and qualify men who I thought might be a good match.

I am not one of those well-preserved, gorgeous,

marathon-running middle-aged women. I have been told I am attractive, but I am overweight and not a gym rat. So while I am active, I do not match the description 90% of men's profiles say they want: slender, athletic, toned, fit. I have some wrinkles — what one sweet suitor mistakenly called dimples. I have what Bridget Jones called "wobbly bits," as most non-surgically enhanced middle-aged women do. My genes — and a lifetime addiction to chocolate — have made their mark. Yet I've met and dated some wonderful men, so even if you're not a lingerie model, you can find guys who will think you're attractive, perhaps even hot!

In my professional life, I am a bestselling author of workplace effectiveness books, professional speaker and management consultant. I've appeared on Oprah, 60 Minutes, and National Public Radio and in the *Wall Street Journal* and *USA Today*.

This book is intended to not only be useful to others and cathartic for me, but is also the genesis of a new topic for fun, thought-provoking speeches. I'm calling myself a dating philosopher and giving date-a-vational speeches! Let me know if you know a group who would like an entertaining after-lunch speech on how lessons learned from dating have implications in business and personal relationships and well as life philosophies.

How did I come by the Dating Goddess moniker? After a few months of dating dozens of men — one week yielded 7 dates with 6 guys in 5 days — my friends dubbed me this name. I liked it, so it stuck.

I'm purposefully not sharing my picture as I don't want you to think either, "How did she get any dates at all?" or the opposite, "Of course she found it easy to get 112 men to ask her out." I am not hideous (usually) nor am I stunning (without professional hair, makeup and Photoshop!). Some men find me attractive, some don't.

I continue to search for my "one," but I have learned a lot along the way, and my single and not-single friends have loudly encouraged me to share my experiences and lessons in the hopes of helping others navigate the adventure of dating with more success. And to have a delicious time doing it!

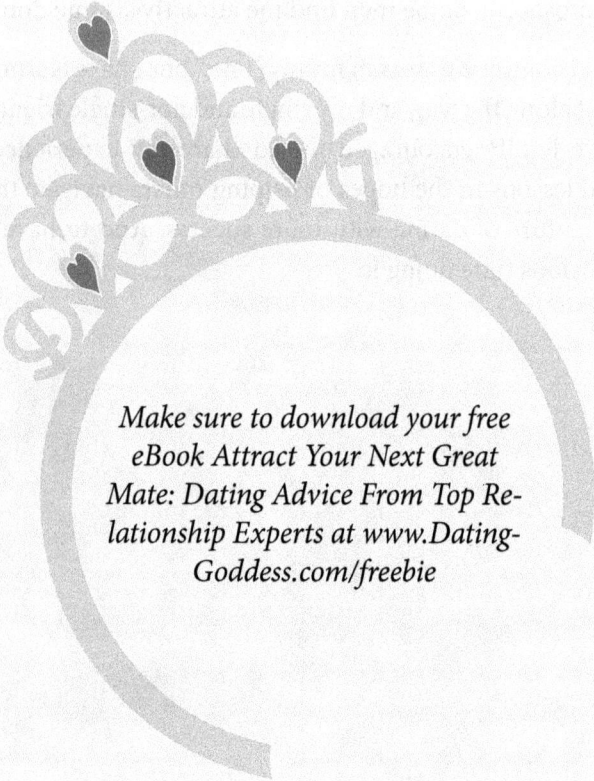

Make sure to download your free eBook Attract Your Next Great Mate: Dating Advice From Top Relationship Experts at www.DatingGoddess.com/freebie

Dating's emotional roller coaster

Your experience dating your current guy swings from elation to disappointment, glee to frustration, fun to hassle. But the good far outweighs the bad, so you stick with it. When it's great, it's really great.

It would be easy to complain about — and to — him. But you have to realize you voluntarily climbed into the front car of this emotional roller coaster. When you look forward to seeing him, you are on the up-hill, raising your hands high in anticipation of a great, adrenaline-filled time with him. If it turns out to be a dud or a difficult time, you are disappointed.

Are you a drama queen? No. Is he a drama king? No. But still there are emotional ups and downs which some find common with new relationships, when you're getting to know each other, having unexpressed — and therefore often unmet — expectations.

In "What's your date's Delight/Disappointment Scale score?" (in the *Real Deal or Faux Beau: Should*

You Keep Seeing Him? book) I suggest you track this relationship's emotional roller coaster route. If there are dramatic highs offset by too many pronounced lows, you are setting yourself up for a world of hurt. Any relationship will have ups and downs. But you want most of your relationship experiences on the upside, and the downs not to repeatedly make your stomach drop.

Should you get off this roller coaster? If after a few weeks things haven't calmed down, then yes. In fact, some people say that any time your emotions go into the Dungeon of Disappointment, you should not overlook the danger signs and sirens sounding. Others believe that you should expect some downs, as no person or relationship is perfect.

But of course, many of us tend to live our dating lives in the Fun House, seeing distorted images of reality. We look in the curved mirror of infatuation and his heart looks unusually big, so that's the image we hold. Even when we step out into the sunlit midway and look at him again, we don't notice that the humongous heart we saw as so large and open is really just normal size. Then we become disappointed when this perceived romantic giant is really a regular guy.

Have you experienced a dating emotional roller coaster? How long did you stay on it? Did you enjoy the ride or hate it? What happened that made you get off?

When your guy vexes you, ask what your highest self would do

When the guy you're dating does something that really torques your jaw, something you consider incredibly rude, self-centered, or insensitive, it's easy to get in his face about it. But if most of the time he's a thoughtful, polite, sharing, caring, conscious guy, this inconsiderate behavior is an anomaly.

So how do you approach the situation with love and maturity, yet let your feelings be known? This concept is not easy to apply when you are in the heat of anger, but when you do the outcome is amazing.

Ask yourself, "What would I do if I were coming from my highest self?"

What do I mean by that? What would you do if you were happy, secure, confident, fulfilled, and at peace with yourself? If you didn't take anything personally, and someone's behavior didn't mean anything about you?

Let's take a dating example. The guy you're dating is commonly late. You've had it. You're ready to lay into him when his sorry self does show up. You get yourself into a rage thinking how disrespectful he is of your time, what a flake he is, why can't he get his life in order, what possibly could take priority over being on time to be with you, and how clearly this shows he's not that into you?

Take a deep breath.

How would you react if you were able to give him some grace? You know he's a kind, considerate, thoughtful guy, and he has an Achilles heel where he tries to do one more thing before leaving, so is often late. When you've talked to him about this, he knows it is a problem and promises to do better, which he has, but he's obviously not cured.

Your highest self forgives him

Your highest self forgives him in advance, and you busy yourself with other things until he arrives. When he does, you matter-of-factly ask if he is alright, as he's a bit later than he said he'd be. He apologizes and says he knows he has a problem with tardiness, and he is working on changing this habit and he

appreciates your patience. You tell him you appreciate his efforts on this because it is bothersome to you when you repeatedly have to wait for him, and you've seen that he's a tad less late than he used to be. You ask him to call you if he realizes he will be late so you can do something else with your waiting time. He agrees, and promises to work hard on changing this behavior.

You feel good about how you handled this because it is in alignment with the self-image you have that you are a kind, understanding, compassionate, patient, calm person.

I practiced this concept of "coming from my highest self" when going through my divorce. My ex was behaving in a way I'd not known him to be in our 20-year relationship. He was making unreasonable demands and insisting on things I didn't think made sense. At first, I got angry, and our mediations deteriorated into shouting matches.

I didn't like how the mediations were turning out. Little got accomplished and I always ended up in tears. I felt disempowered and unable to deal with a man I'd loved for 20 years who was now radically different. I walked out of the sessions with more hurt and anger than when I arrived.

So I tried preparing myself by saying, "I'm going to work at coming from my highest self." When he made an unreasonable demand, instead of getting angry, I began asking him probing questions, "Help me understand why that is important to you?" "You say you want one of our two matched couches. Is it just a couch you want, or do you specifically want that couch?" "If we were to agree on X instead of Y, would that satisfy your need?"

By being more forgiving and calm, I was able to negotiate for what was truly important to me and let go of what wasn't. In fact, I saw it as a gift when he demanded things that I didn't want in my life anymore.

Please don't misunderstand this point — I'm not saying you should put up with abusive, dysfunctional or toxic behavior thinking that is coming from your highest self. Your highest self means you are taking care of you in all ways.

Complain about what you don't have or enjoy what you have

A guy I'd been dating persistently tried to pressure me to go sexually further than I was comfortable. I continued saying "no" and reminded him that he had agreed to my boundaries. He kept commenting on what he'd like to be doing with me. I finally got tired of his trying to persuade me, so said, "You can enjoy what you have or you can complain about what you don't have." I told him we would cease what we were doing if he didn't stop trying to pressure me to go further.

> I realized I needed to take the phrase to heart myself

As I later began to date others, I realized I needed to take the phrase to heart myself. When I find myself complaining about some new love interest not calling as frequently as I'd like, I realize I should just enjoy when we do talk and get together. If I'm not happy that my guy doesn't like to do all the activities I like, I remind myself that I can't expect a mirror-image sweetheart, and I focus on the fun things we both enjoy.

So when you hear yourself complaining about what he doesn't do or say, see if you can turn it around to focus on what he does or says that lights up your heart. Both of you will be so much happier.

The first fight

New relationships frequently end over a first fight. Sometimes there isn't even an actual fight, but one of you says/does/doesn't do something that upsets the other and it's over — without a word ever being a said about it.

So a first fight is important. Not that I'm encouraging you to pick one, but when it happens, look at it as part of the relationship-building process. Of course, you may go for years without having a fight, and I'm not sure if that is good or bad.

Even great relationships involve differences of opinion. Both parties have to be willing to voice their opinions, even if their voices may become agitated in the process. My ex and I rarely fought in 20 years together. I saw this as a sign that we could communicate our differences without getting upset. Only in the divorce mediation did I learn there were lots of things he was upset about but never voiced. So he became passive-aggressive instead. I interpreted his behavior as forgetfulness or moodiness, never identifying it accurately. It would have been better if we'd fought, as the issues would have then been out in the open.

The important parts of a fight to pay attention to are:

Before:

💜 *What triggered it* — Of course you can point to exactly the thing you/he said/didn't say/did/ didn't do. But that is rarely the true cause. This action/inaction is usually a trigger from something from the past. The quicker you realize that and stop acting like it is the current event, the wiser you'll be. And the less prone you'll be to reacting to an ancient trigger. If your ex was always late and didn't apologize then you're going to be more upset with your current beau's tardiness, even if he does apologize.

During:

💜 *What was said* — Was there blaming, name calling, cursing, condescension? Was the anger overblown for the situation? If he calls you despicable names, you know that is a sign of deep anger issues you don't want to be around. Within the first 10 days of dating, the crazy psychiatrist and I had a disagreement and he called me the "b" and the "c" words. I should have ended it then but didn't, and I endured more of his immaturity and unbalancedness until finally we had a fight and I never heard from him again.

💜 *What wasn't said* — No sharing of emotion, no sharing at all — just silence. If he won't talk about how he feels about what happened ("I felt disrespected") and focuses only on the action, you're going to have a hard time understanding what is going on with him. Or if he just gets silent, he's not willing — or doesn't have the skills — to communicate what's happening inside. If he needs a cooling-off period, he needs to tell you so you aren't left wondering why he's clammed up.

💜 *Actions* — Is there stomping, door slamming, leaving in the middle of the fight, ignoring the other? These show that he doesn't know how to deal with anger maturely. However, if he says, "I need some time to cool off so I'm going for a run," accept that he wants to be level headed when you next talk.

After:

💜 *Talking about it* — Did one of you bring up the upset calmly, wanting to discuss what happened? If it's always you, that's a yellow flag. Both of you need to be mature enough to talk about what happened. Were there apologies from both sides? It might have been you that triggered the upset, but if he overreacted or said cruel things, both of you need to apologize. Was there discussion to understand the other's perspective? If it was just brushed under the rug, that's a bad sign.

I find it's not just what a guy gets upset about that tells me a lot about him. It tells me volumes how he fights (or doesn't, thus passive-aggressiveness), as well as what happens afterwards. If a guy isn't willing to talk about it, I know he's not for me. While I'm not always proud of what triggers me, or how I fight, I am always willing to talk about it afterward. If there's no processing of what happened, it doesn't work for me.

If he's willing to discuss it rather than just bailing because it's an uncomfortable conversation, I know he's interested in staying around for a while. The question here isn't, "Are you willing to fight for me?," it's "Are you willing to fight *with* me and trust that we both care enough about the other to stick around to discuss our differences?"

While I haven't had many fights with beaus, the few times it's happened the most common behavior is for him to just disappear afterward. A few have tried to act as if nothing happened. This is not good.

Of course, this knife cuts both ways. If you know you do any of the above (silence, stomping, name calling, etc.), then examine your own behaviors. Perhaps an anger management, assertiveness, or communication class or counseling would be of value to you, as well. Even midlife people don't know how to communicate maturely, especially when they are upset. There are plenty of resources on how to fight fair, but I think you have to practice this skill in a safe environment to learn it, rather than just read about it.

Is he crazy — or are you?

They fell quickly and hard. Within 2.5 weeks of meeting, they were exchanging I love yous. They spent every weekend together and most weekday nights. They were sure they'd found their soul mates. The sex was frequent and fantastic. Then something shifted.

They started fighting frequently. She was often late to their assignations — sometimes 2.5 hours — without informing him. When he called to check on her, the common excuse was "I got caught up in 'Desperate Housewives' (or some TV show)." Did she not know about Tivo? Or that she could watch the episode anytime on abc.com? And isn't it ironic that as she watched the ebbs and flows of romance on the show, she put her own relationship in jeopardy while a hot, enthralling, attentive sweetheart waited for her 10 minutes away?

In their three months dating, she insisted he come to her house for overnights, not because she had kids, but because it was easier on her. She didn't have to pack an overnight bag, nor find parking in his urban neighborhood, even though he had to circle several blocks to do the same in hers. When he expressed his preference to share overnight hosting, she accused him of having commitment issues.

But he felt she was "the one," so suggested they go to couples counseling. Although she had been in therapy before, she insisted he go by himself as it was "his problem, not hers."

A long time ago, a boyfriend tried to convince me that I "really needed counseling." While I'm sure I could have benefited from a trained professional's input, I resented that he didn't see he had any role in the problems we were having. How arrogant to assume an otherwise normally functioning person is to blame for all a relationship's misfires.

In recounting his story, my friend asked, "What do you think? Was I right in ending it, or should I reconsider? Was she crazy or am I?" Knowing him reasonably well, I would not consider him crazy. He's one of the more evolved, intelligent and grounded men I know, who is not afraid of initiating difficult conversations. (He's 10 years younger and I can't convince him he would really like dating an older woman — me!)

How arrogant to assume the other person is to blame for all a relationship's misfires

I responded to his questions that, based on what he told me (acknowledging that I only heard his side of the story), she sounded self-focused and immature, although she is 35 (he's 42). He also shared other examples, and I observed that she made decisions that affected them both and used flimsy reasoning as the basis for her decisions. She became angry when he expressed a different preference. She got upset when he occasionally had work to do on a weekend, yet didn't see a problem when she buried herself under school course work for weekends in a row. She wanted him when she wanted him, and if he wanted to work out or see his friends for a few hours, she'd get upset.

Seem a tad bit controlling to you? You bet! This woman displayed classic self-focused behavior that we sometimes complain about men exhibiting. The controlling virus is present in both genders, of course. I prescribed my friend read "When breaking up is a 'Get Out of Jail Free' card" and, although he broke it off, "How to trump being dumped" (both in the *Moving On Gracefully: Break Up Without Heartache* book).

What do you think? Was he crazy to break up with her? Have you ever been in a similar situation? What did you do?

Pros and cons of expectations

I once read a quote, "The source of all disappointment is unmet expectations." Perhaps unmet hope fits in there too, since all hope isn't an expectation.

In the beginning — and sometimes past the beginning — of a relationship there are unspoken expectations on both sides. You expect he'll treat you with respect, honor your spoken boundaries, make contact frequently and see you regularly.

But what if his expectations of a budding relationship are different? Perhaps "contacting you frequently" for him is every few days and you expect at least once a day? Or "see you regularly" to him means once a week when you'd like at least two times or more? And perhaps he expects intimacy after the third date and you are thinking the third month.

Voicing your expectations is one of the hardest things in a new relationship. You don't want to come across either demanding, needy or clingy. But in the absence of spoken expectations there is only guesswork. He's guessing how to make you happy, and if he guesses right you need to tell him. And if he guesses wrong, you need to help him see what you'd like. And vice-versa.

He's guessing how to make you happy

This involves courage, especially if you really, really like the guy and are concerned your clarity may drive him away if it sounds like demands or neediness. So you have to word it carefully as "I'd like…" or "I have a request…" or "What I'd love from you is…."

I had this lesson recently. A man I've been seeing for three weeks has been the poster man for thoughtfulness, romance, kindness, chivalry. So much so I've dubbed him King Charming. We both tell the other how much we're attracted to the other, how much we like each other, and yes, we even use the "smitten" word. So there's no doubt we're into each other.

Yesterday he asked gently, "What do you want?" I said, "I want as much time with you as possible before I leave on a business trip next week." When we parted, we discussed seeing each other today and that we'd talk to confirm a plan.

He called my cell phone a few minutes before I had

an appointment this morning, and before we hung up he said he'd call me after my appointment. I said I looked forward to seeing him later today. During my appointment he texted me that he was going to have breakfast with a friend, putter around a bit and get some needed things done. He'd call me tomorrow.

Tomorrow?????? What happened to today? Did I misunderstand that we would see each other today? I guess so! Did the cell phone drop out when I said that? When I said, "I want to see you as much as possible before I leave next week" was that not clear that I wanted a lot of time together? So now I'm wondering if I just wasn't specific enough: "I'd like to have dinner together tomorrow night and go for a hike on Sunday." Some gal pals tell me I was too nebulous.

It's true that sometimes what seems clear to you is fuzzy to others. Maybe I didn't use the exact words I think I did. Maybe "See you as much as possible" to him means a few times, or spending a day together. I didn't ask how he interpreted my comment.

Who's responsible for unclear expectations? I think both parties need to take some responsibility. I take responsibility that I wasn't specific enough. When we talk I'll ask him about his understanding.

Expectations — you need to have some, but you also have to have some flexibility if there are hiccups.

Step up or step aside

You have agreed to be exclusive with your beau. But he is not providing all he's agreed to when you each articulated your needs to be exclusive. You've reminded him of the things you said you needed and he said he'd provide. He acknowledges he knows. He does not say he can't give you these things or that they will take time. You've given him what he said he needs. But he isn't consistent with coming through on what is important to you.

But he isn't consistent with what is important to you.

So he has to step up.

And if he won't or can't, he has to step aside.

A "need" is something that you absolutely must have in a relationship. Monogamy. Loyalty. Honesty. Affection. Communication. Sex. Laugher. Respect.

A "want" is something you would really like to have. Flowers. Weekly date nights. Indy movie viewings.

A need is like water, food, air and sleep. If you don't have these, you don't function. In a relationship, needs are the key elements for your satisfaction. Wants are icing on the cake.

If he's not giving you what is essential for you, he's not stepping up. So he has to step aside. If he is emotionally mature, he will realize that if he can't or won't supply what you need from a relationship partner, then he's compelled to step aside. Or if he isn't emotionally mature, you will have to move him aside so you can move on. Don't let your agreement to exclusivity bind you in a relationship where you aren't receiving crucial elements.

What kind of tree are you?

Spending six days with a two-decade-married couple gave me ample opportunity to watch their relationship up close for days on end. Usually when we visit friends or relatives we spend from several hours to a few days with them. When others are around, most of us are on our best behavior. Only after sufficient time do true behaviors and patterns emerge.

I felt a mix of friend, confidant, and behavioral scientist watching their patterns displayed in everyday activities. So when the woman shared some of their hiccups, I began to see where the breakdowns occurred.

A recurring event transpired when one of them suggested doing something his/her way and the other expressed, in an irritated tone, the desire to do it another way. They both sounded irked until one of them acquiesced. The acquiescer, though, showed his/her annoyance, but out of view or earshot of the other.

So the dance continued. These are both highly intelligent people who have worked on their re-lationship. But they con-tinued to repeat patterns of "my way is best" until one gave in. And they wondered why there was resentment.

They wondered why there was resentment

Finally, near the end of my stay, unable to keep quiet any longer, I spoke up.

"You two are both capable, competent and good problem solvers. You seem to get annoyed when the other doesn't see the wisdom of your way of doing something. Rather than realizing that the best solution could be a combination of your ideas, or that either of your fixes would work just fine, you make the other wrong.

"Think of each other like a tree. No, I'm not going all Barbara Walters here —'If you were a tree, what kind of tree would you be?' But let's say you (the guy) are an oak tree. What is great about oaks? They are strong, majestic, and provide acorns which feed wild life. But they aren't very flexible and would not ride out a hurricane very well.

And you (the woman) are like a palm. What is great about palms? They bend in high winds, provide shade from the heat, and create dates or coconuts. But palms survive only in tropical or subtropical weather, so the environment has to be just right to thrive.

"You two go about your life together getting upset that the other doesn't operate like you do. The oak gets upset that the palm is so wishy-washy (flexible) and that her seeds (coconuts) are so big they smash the acorns to bits when they fall. The palm is irritated that the oak is so rigid and his seeds are so tiny you can't find them.

"If you would just step back and appreciate what each of you bring to the party. How each of you is magnificent in your own way, and encourage each other to be more of what you naturally contribute to the relationship. Embrace it and strategically utilize each other's strengths rather than constantly wishing the other were more like you. I think you'd have more peace and love in your relationship, which is what you say you want."

I left shortly after this discussion, so don't know if it made any impact or not. Perhaps this can be a reminder for all of us to appreciate the different strengths each partner brings to the relationship, rather than wishing s/he were more like us.

Have you had success appreciating and embracing your partner's differences rather than condemning them?

Relationship's fate turns on a single response

Our relationship hung on my response to one question in an IM. Depending on how I responded, I would either end the highly passionate but sometimes frustrating relationship or would save it from sudden death and allow us to continue to explore our connection.

It reminded me of the movie "Sliding Doors," starring Gwyneth Paltrow. In it we see how her character's life unfolds both if she catches the subway train home one day and if she does not. Such a seemingly inconsequential event, but the major repercussions are shown in how her life progresses depending on whether she makes it back to her apartment and catches her lover with another woman or not.

Such was a turning point for me with how I answered his question. However, unlike Paltrow's character, I was clear how one answer would play out, but not certain how the opposite answer would.

Have you been conscious of such turning points in

your relationships, where you are confident one choice would lead in one direction, but unclear where the other would lead? You can choose the certainty of one path or the excitement that would follow the second choice. The certain path seems easier because of the predictability, but there is no passion. The uncertain routes where your heart lies, but there is no guarantee of happiness.

His IM followed a few days after several pointed email exchanges, which were not angry and hostile, but directly asked for clarification of behaviors incongruent with words. We were both guilty of inconsistencies that were vexing to the other.

We were both guilty of inconsistencies that were vexing to the other

His IM began: "I am sitting here wondering should we say 'goodbye' here or face to face?" It was an unexpected question based on the previous week's messages which bespoke adoration and attraction. The assumption was that we would say goodbye soon. The question was not "should we say goodbye" but "when and how should we say goodbye."

This was troubling to me as we'd had one of those instant connections — that elusive chemistry. It grew as we got to know each other and were drawn to each other on many levels. But there had been some miscommunications, misunderstandings and unspoken desires.

I knew if I said, "Let's say goodbye now," I would forever close the door on the possibility of exploring if we might indeed be a great partnership. Yes, there had been challenges, but I know few relationships that don't, especially after the initial glow has dimmed a tad. Part of the cause of our miscommunications, I felt, was we didn't spend enough time together to understand each other's thought processes, priorities, and needs. I felt that with a bit more time together, we'd have more information to determine if we were a good match or not. The parts that were good were very, very good, and in my experience of dating, were very rare.

So I said I didn't want to say goodbye, and asked if he did. We had a three-hour IM discussion about our concerns and needs. We worked out some of the issues causing hesitation and agreed to meet to discuss more in person.

I made a choice about which door to close and which to swing open. We don't always have the power of such choice. If he had been insistent on saying goodbye, there would have been little I could have done to keep the door open. And if few of my needs were being met, I would have taken him up on his offer to close the door.

When you are faced with a decision of whether to close or leave open a door on a relationship, look inside and determine if you have had enough of your needs met and if your partner will likely want to give you more, and you to give him what he wants. Don't just take the easy way out by saying goodbye because it looks like working through the issues will be jarring. How you both respond to working through issues tells you a lot about each other and can bring you closer together.

Don't slam the door on a relationship which may have a few rough edges, but that you feel has the potential to be wonderful. Relationships are like diamonds — they need polishing to become resplendent. However, if the relationship is too rocky and causes too much heartache, it is best to close that door so another one can be allowed to open.

You want boo; he wants boo-ty

An Adventures in Delicious Dating After 40 reader writes:

> *I've been dating my 56-year-old boyfriend for six months. I enjoy his company, both in and out of the bedroom, and he says he enjoys mine too. In the beginning, we'd go out to dinner, plays, concerts, movies, picnics, bike rides, etc. Now, he says he has to work late and comes over just to spend the night — including pre-sleep activities, if you know what I mean.*
>
> *I want a boyfriend, not a booty call. When I tell him I want to go out more and do things, he says he knows. He's just overloaded at work now and has to work late and on weekends, so the only time we have to see each other is at night. Uh huh. When I complain a lot, he'll take me out to dinner, but as soon as we are back at the house, he starts seducing me.*

I have no idea if he is working in the evening and weekends, or at home or out with the guys. He only has a cell phone and often doesn't answer. I'm concerned that he just sees me as a f-buddy and is faking the work excuse.

How do I let him know I want more than a sex buddy? I've told him, but he hasn't done much to make me see that he is willing to be with me for more than a roll in the hay.

Interesting dilemma. Do you trust he's telling you the truth and wait out his heavy work schedule, putting aside your needs? Or do you insist that at least some of your needs be met?

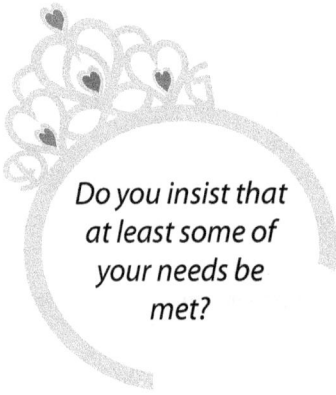

Do you insist that at least some of your needs be met?

Have a heart-to-heart talk with him. Tell him again what your needs are, not in a nagging, complaining way, but straightforwardly. Tell him you love his company and doing things with him beyond the bedroom. Tell him you'd like to experiment with scheduling an activity once a week that doesn't involve a sleepover.

Then wait for his reaction. He may sound amenable in the moment, "Sure sweetie. We can do that. I know it's been difficult on you with my work schedule.

I'll work harder to make sure we go out at least once a week." But then wait until he agrees to the non-booty call part. If he does follow through with an outing each week, see if he expects to stay over afterwards. My guess is he will. If you send him back to his own place, I'd guess he'll begin to pull back all together and not call or see you as much. If so, you have your answer. You are his booty call, not his boo.

Sometimes you have to force his hand to get the answer you need, even if you don't really want it. But if having a relationship beyond the bedroom is important to you, you have to call him out on this. You could go years not getting your needs met waiting for this guy's "heavy work period" to lighten up. And perhaps he's not really at work, just waiting until dark to get you under the sheets.

Make sure to download your free eBook Attract Your Next Great Mate: Dating Advice From Top Relationship Experts at www.Dating-Goddess.com/freebie

"He wants you on his terms"

An older, wiser gal pal and I were talking about relationships, and specifically the one I was in at the time. I was sharing that I loved, loved, loved being with my guy, but his contact between dates was intermittent, and he didn't set future dates beyond the next day. This was vexing, as I am a planner and liked to know when I'd be seeing him so I could schedule friends at other times.

"He is in control. He calls you and sees you when he wants. It is you who asks, 'When will I see you.' It should be the other way around."

She was right. I did ask the question more often, as I wanted to know at least 24 hours in advance. I'd explained to him that I'd like a few days notice, and sometimes he'd comply but mostly it was more spur of the moment.

She continued, "He wants you on his terms — when and where it works for him. While he makes a modicum of effort to appear to address your needs, he really pulls the strings."

"Yes, he wants me on his terms. But I think we all want our relationship on our own terms. We want what we want. None of us gets 100% of what we want. That's why compromise is so critical. If only one of you is compromising, then the power is unbalanced. One of you will feel put upon and disrespected."

The key is to be cognizant of how much compromising each of you is making to keep it somewhat in balance. However, I've noticed it's much easier to note what compromises you've made, as you're less aware of the ones he's made. When you observe his attempts at compromise, it's important to acknowledge that you appreciate his working to find a common ground or give you what you want.

My friend pointed out that control issues can lead to abuse issues, so to watch out. I can see how that could be true, although it was interesting to observe potentially controlling behavior in another, as my ex accused me of being controlling.

What do you think the balance is for each person to feel s/he is getting the relationship on his/her own terms? How do you know when you are compromising too much?

Noticing what's positively eliminated

In relationships — even dating relationships — you often discover behaviors in the other that drive you batty. These behaviors aren't deal breakers, just minor annoyances. So you non-judgmentally share your irritation with your guy and ask him if he would be willing to work on reducing this. He is accommodating, apologizes for it whatever it is that irks you, and says he'll work on it.

Let's say his irksome behavior is poking you in the ribs when he's teasing you about something. You don't really mind the teasing, but it's the poking that smarts a bit, so you tell him. He agrees to be more conscious and stop doing it.

A few days pass. He says something teasingly. No poke. But you don't notice the absence. The next day he teases you, along with a poke. "You did it again. I told you to stop poking me!" He apologizes and says he's working on it. Another day, another teasing; no poke. And another. The next one is a teasing/poking combo.

"You must not care that this irritates me because you're still doing it!"

"I'm sorry. I've been really working on this. It's an old habit we've done in my family for decades. It will take a little time for me to undo it."

You haven't noticed what's missing — the poke. You only notice when it's still present, not the times it's absent.

This is human nature. Congratulations. You're part of the human race.

The hard part with any requested behavior change is noticing progress when that improvement is actually the absence of something. It's hard to notice when something is no longer there, unless you're really conscious.

I remember many years ago deciding to severely limit my cursing, which previously had been liberal. My ex and I had discussed how it sounded unprofessional and unladylike when I would let loose a curse word, when a non-curse word would suffice. At first it sounded a little silly to say "drat," "darn," and "sugar" instead of the more profane versions, but I made a huge effort to utter these. However, an expletive would occasionally leak out and my ex would hear it. He didn't notice that I'd eliminated 90% of my cussing, and only heard the few swear words and thought I hadn't made much progress.

So when you ask your guy to make a shift to eliminate some vexing behavior, be sure you notice the progress. Sometimes absence is progress.

He doesn't introduce you to his adult kids

An Adventures in Delicious Dating After 40 reader asks:

> I'm a single woman with three grown children, ages 26, 24, and 19, all on their own. I've been dating a man for eight months who has two adult sons, ages 37 and 35. He is fearful of introducing them to me, although he's met my children (and liked them), friends, and we are now planning a trip to my brother's home. I really love him but am concerned that he will continue to hide our relationship — one son knows he is dating, but not my name or anything about me. How could I support him in introducing us, and after a year, should I write him off if he's taken no action?

Interesting question. I became sensitive to some people's concern about introducing a new love to their kids when a man I dated for seven weeks cited as a reason for breaking up my suggesting we take his college-aged kids to dinner. Within a week he broke up with me. There were no other clear issues that would have caused this — we got along well. But who knows if this was a smokescreen or there were other doubts he wasn't voicing.

I know folks with minor-aged kids often don't like to have the people they're dating meet their kids before they have a sense that this new love will be in their lives for a while. They say it's damaging to the kids to get attached to someone then have the wo/man out of their lives because of a breakup.

While your guy's kids are much older, perhaps he is protecting them or you. One man shared that his adult kids hated every woman he'd introduced to them after his divorce — even almost a decade afterward! They harbored the fantasy that mom and dad would get back together, so they didn't want to encourage dad to have a new love interest. They commonly said things to dad's dates, like "I'll never like you." This damaged some of his relationships with women who didn't understand it had nothing to do with them. So maybe your guy is postponing an uncomfortable altercation but isn't telling you the reason.

His adult kids hated every woman he'd introduced to them

I'm guessing you've said things like, "I'd love to have

your kids meet my kids on the next college break," or "Let's have your sons over for (dinner, the next holiday, or a fun outing)."

I heard a relationship expert say that men need a nine-month gestation period for a serious relationship — at least for him to realize he wants a serious relationship with a specific woman. If this is true, you're just at eight months. I'd try the subtle approach until the nine-month mark (although I realize most men like directness and miss a lot of subtlety). Then I'd have a serious discussion with him, something like, "I've suggested we get together with your sons several times. I'm wondering if there's a reason you don't want us to meet each other right now?"

Where's the line between getting your needs met and being selfish?

Midlife daters generally have more experience in relationships and thus negotiating solutions to different relationship desires. However, if you have been unpartnered for a number of years, you are probably used to getting what you want because you haven't had to take an adult partner's desires into account.

So let's say you (or your guy) want something. The other wants something different. Ideally, you find a compromise — without resenting the other. But that is not always possible.

For example:

♥ You want him to attend your niece's college graduation at which she will be speaking as class president. You would get to introduce him to some favorite out-of-town relatives who are only in town for the day. The same day — during the same time — he wants you to attend an old friend's wedding. He wants to show you off and for you to meet his old friends. You would know no one but him and the groom, whom you don't really like. These are both once-in-a-lifetime events. You can't attend both, and neither of you are thrilled about the prospect of attending either event alone or with someone other than your sweetie. Because of logistics you can't attend part of one then go to the other.

♥ You're both astronomy buffs. A meteor shower you both want to see will soon be visible in your area. You want to camp out overnight on a mountaintop as it will offer the best darkened view, plus will be romantic. He wants to pitch the tent in his suburban back yard as it will be easier, and he says it will be dark enough to see most of the meteor streaks.

What if your scenario's options are win/lose? One of you must compromise, and there is not a solution that would allow you both to get enough of what you want to be satisfying.

One of you can say, "You have your way this time and I'll get mine

What if your scenario's options are win/lose?

next time." Or, if it is really, really important to you, you may propose, "I know your option/situation/event is important to you. Mine is really important to me. We aren't seeming to come up with a compromise. If you'd be willing to let me have what I want this time, I promise you can have your way next time."

Are you being selfish to request this? Or just trying to get your needs met?

If the trade-off frequency is uneven, with one of you compromising more often, then the power is not equally shared. You both deserve to get what you want half the time if it appears there is an impasse.

I've found you can sometimes invent a creative solution if both of you are willing to try — and not be wedded to getting 100% of your way. If you are willing to discuss what is important to you and what you want, you may be able to find a solution that has the most important elements for each of you. This is not always possible, of course, but it is worth a try.

The key for me, however, is the willingness to initiate a compromise. If both of you argue you will only be happy with 100% of what you want, then there is no room for negotiation. Or if neither of you is willing to suggest discussing options, it's a lose/lose. And if one of you always initiates a compromise, that is lopsided, too.

If I were in scenario #2, I would ask my guy what is important about staying close to home. He might say, "I can't sleep in a tent very well. If it were in my back yard, I could go inside when it became uncomfortable and sleep in my bed. I'd have a bathroom and refrigerator nearby." Knowing that, I could suggest, "I see your considerations. Would you be willing to have us go up to the mountain top until a little past midnight, when the most meteors show up, then have us drive home or to a nearby hotel to sleep the rest of the night?"

If you are voicing your needs and not getting them met, you need to discuss this with your guy. Perhaps he's not comfortable negotiating. Or perhaps he doesn't know it's important. And you need to be clear that sometimes some of what you want is better than none of what you want. At least some of the time.

Expressing your upset with your guy

When conflict occurs in a personal relationship, it's easy to blame the other. In my communication seminars I teach a 4-step method* for telling someone you're upset with something they've done or said.

First, you describe the situation. "The toilet seat was left up again." "You were 30 minutes late for our date." "You said you'd call yesterday and you didn't."

The second step is "Express how you feel." We give the participants the sentence stem, "When you …, I feel …." Even after explaining that the "I feel" part is for you to express your emotion — frustrated, upset, sad, disrespected, disappointed, etc. — people typically tend to twist this into blaming: "I feel you don't really care what I want," "I feel you're lazy," "I feel you're just not trying very hard." This is called "mind reading" as you really don't know what's going on in the other person's mind unless you ask. So unless you're a psychic, avoid mind reading!

Thirdly, you specify what you want to happy. "I'd appreciate it if you'd work harder at putting the toilet seat down." "I would like you to do whatever you need to do so you aren't late again." "I want you to be more rigorous about honoring your promises."

And last, communicate the consequences. "I'm be in a much better mood if you arrive on time so we can make the start of the movie."

A formula or technique can be easy to understand and easy to practice in a classroom role play. It's quite another thing when you are in the heat of the moment with someone you care about. Your training and knowledge seem to easily fly out the window. It's happened to me even though I teach the method! It can take all your focus when you're emotionally plugged in to put into practice something you know well, as your ability is impaired to detach enough to search your knowledgebase and act calmly and rationally.

Your training and knowledge seem to easily fly out the window

So what to do? Ideally, when you find yourself getting too emotionally upset to think clearly, you express that you need to take a breather to compose your thoughts. Don't just walk away or hang up, but explain what you're doing. Again, I haven't practiced what I

preach 100% of the time and I am upset with myself when I don't implement what I know works.

The concept of taking a breather is called "buying time." You tell him, "I want to resolve this, but I'm not thinking clearly now. I'm going to take a walk around the block and we can pick this up in 15 minutes." It gives both of you a chance to think through what you're feeling, how to express it and what you want to happen. Sometimes you may need a day or two. Let him know you aren't just abandoning the conversation or bailing on him.

Stating a reconvening time frame is important. Otherwise it is too easy to just go away and either not come back or pretend nothing has happened. Then the resentment just festers. It feels like this isn't an important issue. And while it may not be important to one of you, if it's important to the other it should be given attention from both out of respect for the one who brought it up.

What have you found works when you're having an emotionally charged conversation (e.g., fight) with the guy you're dating?

The method is called the DESC Script. This stands for Describe, Express, Specify (what you want to happen), and Consequences (state what positive will happen if the change happens). This method was developed by Sharon and Gordon Bower.

Are you expecting a wild horse to act tame?

An Adventures in Delicious Dating After 40 reader writes:

> The middle-aged man I've been seeing for a few months is Mr. Spontaneity. He rarely plans anything in his life more than a day in advance, including our getting together. Last week he called me as he was leaving his house — 45-minutes away — and asked if I would have lunch with him. Luckily, I could swing it. I've told him I'd like at least a day's notice, but he doesn't seem to be able to shift his mind from the here and now. I considered saying "no" to lunch just to show him I'm not always available, but I wanted to see him, and to say no when I was available seemed game playing.

> Last night I'd been invited to a small dinner party and invited him to accompany me. I'd told him about it last week and reminded him again a few days ago. He said he had to check his calendar

and he'd get back to me. He never did. I texted and called him before I left for the event, but I only heard from him an hour ago. He'd gone out of town to visit friends for the weekend, without a word to me.

I was livid thinking how disrespectful this was to not let me know he wouldn't be attending. When we are together he is the epitome of respectful, kind, and attentive. But when we're not, he doesn't call or text for a few days. We've discussed how neither of us is interested in seeing others, so I don't think another woman is taking his focus. I'm not sure what to do. I want to have someone I can depend on to attend social functions, not a fly-by-night lover.

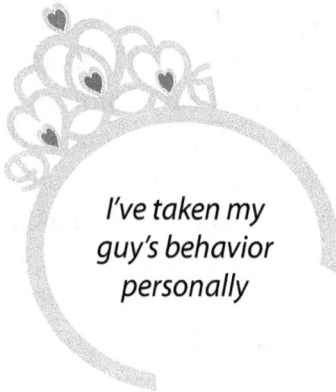

> I've taken my guy's behavior personally

I've been there before, taking my guy's behavior personally and getting huffy at the perceived slights. It is easy and natural to do. You have to decide if it is just a difference in styles or if he is taking you for granted. If the former, you have to ask yourself if you are willing to shift your expectations, as it is doubtful he will change.

He sounds like he is like a wild stallion, coming and going at his whim, running where his interests take him. Occasionally, he will come to you for the sweet sugar you provide. You want him to be like the corralled horse: predictable, stable, and tamed. Perhaps part of his allure is his wildness and unpredictability, as well as the quality of your experience with him — when he nuzzles you, you know there is no where else on the planet he'd rather be. He focuses on you completely — until he's off again for a few days, sowing his wild oats.

The corralled horse also has appeal. You know you can count on him, you can lead him where you want, you know where to find him at all times. He's happy in his pen as long as it includes regular attention and feeding from you. But some women find this kind of relationship boring.

You are expecting your guy to act boyfriend-like. But he is, it seems, unwilling to be tamed. If your irritation at his spontaneity overwhelms your love of spending time with him, then move on. But if you like to be with him and need some predictability, then consider renegotiating your exclusivity and agree to see others. You will, no doubt, find someone who is more traditional in his interest and ability to commit to a social engagement a week or two in advance. As long as all parties know there is not an exclusivity agreement, then you can see two people at once. It may not be optimal, but since your wild horse is not likely to change his ways, you need to explore options for getting your needs met. Yelling at and nagging him won't accomplish what you want. A wild horse will buck off an unwelcomed rider, and you will not enjoy the experience.

Should you take him back?

An Adventures in Delicious Dating After 40 reader writes:

> *I recently dated a guy for a few months but then we had a falling out. We tried to discuss it by email and phone since we were both traveling and we couldn't meet face-to-face. We set a time in a few days to meet to discuss if we should continue. I have mixed feelings, as I really like being with him and he has many, many characteristics I am looking for in a man. But he would go for a week with no contact which made me feel I wasn't a priority in his life.*
>
> *How can I determine if I should take him back?*

Good question. You've only been seeing each other a few months, so the relationship is still budding. Most people don't have the strong bond it takes to work things out at this point, but if you do, great.

Be clear what you want. What do you need/want to be different if you decide to continue? Get specific, not just, "I want us to see each other more," but "I'd like for us to see each other at least two times a week, at least

one of which is outside
the house doing some-
thing fun like the beach,
a movie or play, and/
or dinner." Or not, "I'd
like to talk more often,"
to "I want to talk on the
phone at least once per
day at bedtime, and am
open to texts and IMs in
addition."

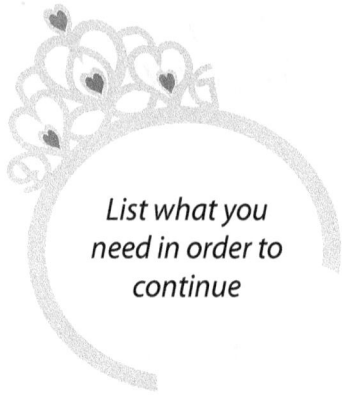

*List what you
need in order to
continue*

List what you need in order to continue. Don't read
this list as demands but more as your desires. Some of
them may be longer term, like, "I want to build our relationship with the intention that we would like to be
together long term."

Of course, you want him to tell you what he wants
as well, not just what he thinks you want to hear. If there
are non-negotiables, then you each need to say that. If
he says, "I want to see other women," and you say, "I
want to be exclusive," one of you has to give or walk. If
neither of you will compromise, then you need to decide to keep it more casual or call if off. It is hard to
force someone to be exclusive if they don't want to be,
so whoever wants the exclusivity may find it easier to
agree to see others with some caveats. If you say, "We
can both see others but not have sex with anyone else,"
and he doesn't agree, that can be a deal breaker for you.

The keys are to be candid and honest about what
each of you truly wants and to be clear on your deal

breakers. You have to be willing to share what you like about each other, yet be clear you should walk away if you aren't willing/able to give each other most of what you want.

You can also have a trial period to test the waters. "I'm willing to be exclusive for a month, remove myself from all dating sites, end any conversations with past and potential love interests. Then we will discuss how each of us is feeling." Or, "For the next month I'm willing to go out to dinner with your friends twice if you will go out with mine twice."

Romantic relationships seem to be a constant stream of compromises. The key to feeling good is to have each of you be willing to 1) discuss what you want in a non-demanding way, 2) offer a compromise, 3) not hold a grudge if you agreed to concede.

DatingGoddess.com

Is his toothbrush in your cabinet too soon?

Does the guy you're dating leave personal items at your place — without asking?

Two men have done this at my house. The latest was after a second sleepover, but unbeknownst to me. During his third visit I asked if he wanted a toothbrush or if he brought one. He said, "I left one here last time. I've taken over the empty shelf in your bathroom." "Really?" I thought, "Kinda presumptuous don't you think?" But I bit my tongue, as I really didn't mind. I just thought it was interesting that he would move in his toiletries so quickly and without any discussion, let alone permission. I don't think I'd be so assumptive.

Yet I knew he hungered for some sense of permanency between us, so I didn't mind a toothbrush, comb, razor and deodorant occupying my formerly empty shelf. In fact, it was unoccupied because I didn't use that bathroom much. "So what's the harm?" I thought.

As it turns out it was indicative of bigger issues and

assumptions. He was more bent on our living together than I was. He longed for me to make a commitment to him even though we'd known each other only a few months. This ultimately colored both of our expectations of the relationship and each other.

He saw my lack of interest in moving to his area — 600 miles away — as a sign that I was selfish and he surmised he'd have to move to mine, live in my house, sit on my furniture, and eat my food. Interesting, since none of this was ever discussed, so it was all his assumption. I felt 2-3 months of dating was way too soon to know if the relationship should continue, let alone be semi-permanent. He saw my insistence that it was too early as rejecting him. Which in a way, I was — rejecting my willingness at this time to work toward permanence with a man I felt I hardly knew.

> *He saw my insistence that it was too early as rejecting him*

The other beau left clothing on my bedroom chair in between weekend sleepovers. I'm a neat person, so this bothered me. I suggested he keep them in an empty drawer — perhaps like the man described above, in an attempt to create a sense of permanence. But similarly, it was too soon to assume a bond. His clothing should have left each time he did. When we had our final clash on the phone, his clothes were still at my place. I should have told him to fetch them or donated them to Goodwill, but I called to tell him I'd drop them off since I was going to his neighborhood. He never returned the call, so I left the bags on his doorstep. Even how this got resolved was indicative of our relationship — he became uncommunicative when he didn't get his way; I tried to make nice and show there were no hard feelings even though our last fight was over his trying to manipulate me.

So what have I learned? That both parties should keep their belongings with them and not leave items at the other's abode. It takes some effort to schlep your stuff back and forth, but it is better for the relationship. You don't want to leave your baggage — emotional or physical — at someone else's house.

Make sure to download your free eBook Attract Your Next Great Mate: Dating Advice From Top Relationship Experts at www.Dating-Goddess.com/freebie

Do you infantilize your guy?

Infantilize: Treat (someone) as a child or in a way that denies their maturity in age or experience.

"Does he want a 'mommy'?" (in the *In Search of King Charming: Who Do I Want to Share My Throne?* book) discussed how some men want a woman who will take care of them. Let's talk about the flip side — women who treat the midlife man they're dating (or married to) like a child.

Perhaps she doesn't do it all the time, but sometimes — occasionally — she questions his judgment, or treats him like he doesn't know what he's doing. He may be successful at work, making important decisions, yet in their relationship she frequently second guesses or criticizes his decisions.

If you're the one doing it, you're not usually aware you are. And when it is pointed out, a common rationale is, "I'm just trying to help." Maybe you have evidence (at least to you) that he hasn't made good decisions in this area in the past, or you generalize that men don't make good choices around this (e.g., appearance or decorating), or you have some experience from the last man/men you've been with who have not done this particular thing well.

I'm not proud to admit that I have some experience infantilizing a man or two (and probably more). I have all sorts of justifications for why I question his past, present or future decision. And yes, I usually defend my egregious behavior with the aforementioned, "I'm just trying to help." I was convinced I was, although the outcome, of course, was 180 degrees from helpful.

Here's a recent example. A man I dated exclusively for three months and I were on a weekend getaway. He wanted to buy a pair of swim trunks as we planned to relax in the hotel hot tub that evening. I was to accompany him, erroneously believing he wanted my input. At the first store, he chose a pair labeled "large" and said "This should fit." My ex wore a large and he weighs 50 lbs less than Mr. Romantic. I suggested, "Let's hold it up to your waist and see if it will work." I did and it was definitely too small, as was an XL. We went to another store.

This time the trunks were tagged with waist sizes. He grabbed one labeled with his measurement and said, "This will do" and started toward the cashier. I suggested, "Don't you want to try it on?" He said, "No. This is my size." Feeling that since just moments ago he thought he was a large and clearly wasn't, and knowing he'd lost a large amount of weight recently, perhaps he was a little fuzzy on his current size. I held up the chosen trunks to his waist and they, too, didn't look like they'd fit. "I really think you should try them on," I said, thinking I was being helpful.

Now you, astute reader, already know that this was not received as helpful. It was heard as bossy, mothering, condescending, and yes, infantilizing. He glared at me. Then he stomped towards the fitting room. A few minutes later he beelined past me when I asked if they fit. Back at the swim suit rack he grabbed another pair and marched toward the cashier, with nary a word to me. (See "The first fight," page 9, for lessons from this encounter.)

He later explained that if he bought the wrong size, he would just return them or buy another pair. My attitude was

1) that would be a waste of money as swim suits aren't usually returnable,

2) we drove an hour to this store from our seaside resort and it would be doubtful we'd return that evening if they didn't fit, and

3) if he didn't have trunks that fit, he couldn't accompany me to the hot tub, which would be less fun for both of us.

Serendipitously, a month later his 22-year-old daughter had a nearly identical experience with her boyfriend. They were swim trunk shopping and he grabbed a pair. She suggested (insisted?) he try them on, and he was incensed that she thought he didn't know what size he wore.

Now some of this is chalked up to women's experience trying on clothes and having the same size fit completely differently from one manufacturer to another. Because of this, women nearly always try on clothing before purchasing, and wouldn't think of buying a swim suit before trying it on, no matter how psychically painful. Also, when women shop together it's commonplace to try on something and get the other's opinion, who often helpfully points out it pulls over the rump, or the color makes you look jaundiced. Men have a very different experience of shopping, it seems.

This example helps us understand why women treat men in ways that men interpret as condescending. (I know men also infantilize women, but we will save that for another discussion.) And perhaps it's just part of Venus and Mars and we should all just reread John Gray's classic book.

While not all patronizing behavior is designed to "help," some of it is. The other justification women use to explain why they treat a man like a child is that he is acting childlike! A pal recently shared that her 50ish date refused to put on his seat belt. Men I've dated have behaved in ways reminiscent of adolescence. If they are going to act like a child, it is hard to resist treating them like one! But of course, they are men and know the consequences of their actions, so why would we take it upon ourselves to try to suggest their behavior is immature?

Because we're trying to help!

Before agreeing to a weekend getaway, clarify expectations

I told an out-of-town guy I'd been seeing occasionally for seven months that I was coming to his area for business. He said, "Why don't you stay for the weekend and we can go away somewhere?" That sounded good to me. Since although we talked daily, we hadn't seen each other in a few months, I was envisioning a romantic get away.

"Sounds good. Where will we go?"

"There's a resort I like about 90 minutes from my place. It's beautiful there."

Now it sounded even better. I made my flight arrangements.

A week before the trip, I asked, "So I know what to pack, what activities do you imagine we will be doing?"

"We'll have dinner Friday, then I'm playing golf on Saturday."

"Really?" I asked incredulously. This was the first mention of golf, and since he knows I'm not a golfer I asked, "And what shall I do while you golf?"

"Anything you want!"

So this "romantic" weekend was really an excuse for him to play golf and me to tag along. While I am perfectly capable of entertaining myself, I was taken aback by his cavalier attitude. He clearly didn't see any problem with him taking nearly a day out of our short tryst to go off on his own.

I'd asked the "And what shall I do while you golf?" question to see if he'd given any thought to his leaving me out of his Saturday plans. Clearly, he had not. If he had, he would have responded with something like, "You could have a massage at the spa, work out, go shopping, read by the pool. There are lots of activities onsite that you enjoy. I've asked the concierge to give us a map and list of local activities if you want to explore the town in my car. And they have a special spa day package I'm happy to give you if you want to do that while I golf."

> *So this "romantic" weekend was really an excuse for him to play golf*

Or I would have felt differently if he'd broached it by saying, "I know we'll only have a few days together and we haven't seen each other for a long time. I'm looking forward to spending time with you. However, I have one favor to ask. Would you mind terribly if I took an early tee time on Saturday, as this resort has one of my favorite courses? I'd be back to take you to a great lunch and do anything you want together the rest of the day. And you're welcome to use my car if you want to tour the town that morning."

I realize I should have asked more of the "What do you envision us doing?" questions when he first tendered the invitation. Then I would have known what his idea of a weekend getaway together was, and could have had input then or declined the invitation.

I toyed with confronting him with my being taken aback. But the more I thought about it, I felt that this was to be the make-or-break weekend. I wanted to see how he thought about me, us and how he behaved without input or guidance from me. While I believe in speaking up and being clear on what you want, a guy has to have some basic values that you like, without your continually guiding him, or you'll feel like a nag. Inclusiveness, consideration and thoughtfulness seem pretty basic, don't they?

I own that it was my expectation that this was to be a romantic weekend. I made that assumption without asking about his expectations, either. So we both made assumptions without clarifying them with the other.

Teed off by weekend getaway with golf addict

In "Before agreeing to a weekend getaway, clarify expectations," I told you of a weekend "romantic" getaway with a man I'd seen occasionally over seven months. A week before the outing, he sprang on me that he planned to golf Saturday. I was not pleased, but I was willing to be a good sport, under the premise (and promise) that we'd spend time together doing other activities.

The weekend's opening act didn't bode well. When he picked me up from the airport, there was no hug or kiss. He scurried to throw my luggage into his trunk and turned to get back in the car. I caught him and kissed him on the cheek. No stopping for an embrace or a lip lock. No "I'm glad to see you" or "I'm looking forward to spending the weekend with you."

The 90-minute drive to the resort took 2.5 hours in heavy traffic. The resort was nice but offered no other sport options but golf. I'm not a golfer.

After we checked in I thought we'd have dinner in

the restaurant, since earlier in the week he said we'd dine out on Friday. Instead, he said we'd have room service. I guess since we were out of his apartment, that was "out" in his mind! But I'm flexible. He'd had a hard week. We watched TV until he fell asleep.

Saturday he arose early for his tee time. Before he left I confirmed he'd be back between 11:00 and noon. He said, yes, he would. I busied myself with a walk, checking email, chatting with the concierge, and reading. I made sure I was back in the room by eleven.

He returned nearly an hour late, without letting me know

He returned nearly an hour late, without letting me know. When I told him I'd expected him by noon, he said he'd told me it would be closer to 1:00. Hmmm, I had no memory of that information. We drove to a nearby town for lunch. Back in the room, he took a nap. I took a walk. Since we had a big lunch we didn't want much dinner, so we snacked while watching an in-room movie.

Sunday it rained. He said if it hadn't, he would have golfed. That would have been cause for a pointed discussion about why he bothered to bring me on this getaway.

Arriving back at his apartment, he turned on the TV to watch … golf! I went for a walk. I was taking a lot of walks by myself this weekend. When I returned, the tournament was over so I told him there were several movies nearby that I wanted to see and their start times. He said we should see if there was a TV movie to watch, and found one — featuring golf! I read while he watched it. We watched TV from opposite sides of the couch the rest of the evening.

So the weekend with this golf addict shanked. He had no concept of how to be flexible and do some of what I wanted, although I felt I was clear. He did what he would have done if I hadn't been there, and he didn't give a nanosecond of thought to what I might like to do or how to make me happy during this rare weekend together. I could have made more of a ruckus, but when I did say what I wanted or made suggestions, he ignored me or chose to do something else. I used this time as an experiment to see if he thought at all of my enjoyment or only his own.

I hit this guy out of bounds — where he's staying.

What did I learn?

💟 Clarify your expectations ahead of time. Ask about possible activities to be done singly and together.

💟 In any weekend getaway, some alone time is not a bad thing. However, if the weekend is to help you get to know each other better, spending too much time on individual activities does not accomplish this goal.

💜 Watching TV together can be a way to relax and snuggle. But if it dominates your time together, you're not getting to know each other at all.

💜 Trust your intuition. I used this weekend as a bit of a test to see if he was more thoughtful than he seemed on the phone. I needed some final evidence to convince myself to let him go. He ended up being less considerate than the last time we saw each other. I was hoping he would be more thoughtful, but now I knew that is not who he is or how he thinks. So I've released him for some other woman who has different needs than mine — and who golfs!

Sharing your dating disclaimer

A friend, a long-time dater and avowed bachelor until he met his soul mate several years ago, had a printed dating disclaimer. He says he made women read it before he slept with them. He says,

"I know it's bizarre, but I wanted them to know what they were in for."

What was in his disclaimer? Here's what it said:

As we take another step forward...

To avoid any possibility of you feeling misled in the future, I want to offer some "full disclosure" on several points. You may well think this is way premature, and I agree. I just want you to know up front what's up with me. If you find something below that you don't like about me, you can bail right now. I'm completely open to talking about anything. If you have questions, ask away. I have no sensitive areas.

♥ **Shopping** — *My very favorite store is Costco and I go there frequently. I'm not likely to ever become a Nordstrom repeat customer. Most of what I wear and eat comes from Costco. If the chic "Kirkland" brand turns you off, well, you should know I'm not likely to stop shopping there, and that I even get a little thrill each time I even drive past a Costco.*

♥ **Age** — *I told you that I have 99% integrity and that I would always let you know if I were in the 1% zone. Well, I'm 53, not 49 as I showed in my profile. It may well make a difference to you that I'm "in my fifties" or that I did tell this one lie. If so, I completely understand. The fact is that there's quite a stigma attached to being "in your fifties." I don't feel 50, I don't act 50, people say I don't look 50, but I am "in my fifties." There's absolutely not one single other fact or statement that has come up during our "getting acquainted" process that is untrue. Nor will there be.*

♥ **Children** — *In case there is any lingering possible remote teeny thought in your mind that you'd like to be with a man who might start a family with you some time in the distant future, you should know that I've had a vasectomy. It's certainly not that I thought you might be trying to trick me into fathering a child. It's just that I know some women have secret lingering maternal urges and I don't want you to waste any time with me if that's something you would like in your future.*

💜 *Marriage Prospects* — *If your true aim is to find a man who will court you, propose to you, and then marry you, I'm probably not a good bet. I look upon life as a series of fascinating adventures. I've had great relationships in the past with spectacular friends and lovers.*

💜 *Sometimes relationships with girlfriends have gone sour when it becomes clear that I'm not really looking for a marriage partner or life-mate. I don't rule out that possibility forever, and at the same time I just don't see it in my medium-term future.*

💜 *Money* — *I like friends and lovers to have some mutual financial involvement in their relationships. I'm not one of those "old fashioned guys" who would be insulted if you picked up the tab for coffee now and then. I have no financial shortage, and it's not the amount involved that matters to me. If we go out for some lavish feast and I pay, and later you buy an iced tea, I consider that "even." I don't ever need for you to "keep up" with me in dollar terms. You should know, though, that I don't like it when I buy everything. Just pay for coffee now and then and I'm happy. I don't like feeling that I'm on a one-way street.*

💜 *Religion* — *I'm an agnostic. Various people have different interpretations of what that means. Webster's my authority: a person who holds the view that any ultimate reality (as God) is unknown and prob. unknowable; broadly: one who is not committed to believing in either the existence or the nonexistence of God or a god.*

That's exactly how I see things. The "spiritual" interpretation I have of the world is abhorrent to many with conventional religious views. It would be intellectually arrogant of me to insist that my view is right, and that Catholics or Muslims or anybody else is wrong. I don't know about God, and I don't think anybody does or can know. Generally speaking, scientific, rational, Darwinian theorems always carry the most weight with me.

Monogamy *— In my whole life, I have never been unfaithful to a girlfriend or wife. During this odd online dating process, I imagine that both of us will be meeting a variety of people. One thing I will not ever do is put you in a situation where your health is at any risk. Oh, by the way, I'm in perfect health in every respect including sexual health. In the last year, I've had intercourse with two girlfriends, and have had a complete blood test prior to being that intimate, and insisted that my lover did, too. I'm ultra cautious about my health.*

Sensuality *— Should it happen that we eventually become intimate, you should know that I'm not one of those Neanderthal caveman types who just wants to grunt and screw (sorry). I care more about touching, caressing, tasting, kissing, and laughing. I was a hippie type guy in the 1970s and* *have lingering tendencies. Nudity and the beautiful human body don't bother me in the least. I've had a girlfriend with a mastectomy, one with secret piercings, and so on. I'm not scared of that stuff. And I like giving massages as much as receiving.*

Openness — *Just about nothing embarrasses me or makes me want to change the topic. You can ask me anything and I'll give you a completely candid answer. Or, I'll tell you that my answer isn't truthful, like the age deal. Ask what you want to know. I didn't write this to avoid talking to you about these things, but to stimulate talking about them. I want to be sure you're fully informed about me.*

So, what should I know about you along these lines?

What would you put in your disclaimer?

How to introduce your midlife flame to colleagues?

My sweetie at the time and I were talking about a function we would be attending with his professional colleagues. He asked, "How shall I introduce you to my associates and co-workers? What shall I call you? I want to tell them of our relationship when I introduce you as my — what?"

> *We wanted to use the right word that was not too familiar and not too formal*

We wanted to use the right word that was not too familiar and not too formal, but also expressed our relationship properly.

81

We debated the options. "Girlfriend" seemed a too juvenile for a 51-year-old woman. "Lover" was too explicit. "Main squeeze" too base. "Friend" too distant. "Date" too cold. It was too early in our relationship to be considered his "significant other." "Sugar," "sweet baboo," "lady love" and "honey" all a tad too informal for professional colleagues. We decided "sweetie" or "sweetheart" sounded fine.

Now, what was I to call him when I introduce him to my circle? "Boyfriend" was out for the same reason "girlfriend" wasn't right. "Suitor" was fine in writing, but sounded stilted verbally. "Fella" sounded out of date. "Escort" was too remote. "Companion" was a little closer, but without the closeness we feel. "Partner" was pre-mature. "Boy toy" would elicit a laugh, but it is too suggestive for a professional environment. "Swain" and "gentleman caller" were archaic. "Paramour" has a nice ring to it, but the definition is "a lover, especially the illicit partner of a married person." No, that will not do.

"Beau" has a nice ring to it, as does the aforementioned "sweetie" or "sweetheart." So I'll use one of those.

When you've introduced your man to your co-workers or professional colleagues, what adjective did you use? How did you determine what sounded right? Have you ever used a term that your guy didn't like?

Meet the ... kids!

The film "Meet the Parents" showed how nerve wracking it can be to meet your sweetie's parents. Well, how about when you meet his kids? That can be similarly unnerving, since if they don't like you it can strain the relationship.

I had the opportunity to meet one beau's young-adult kids. And while there was a little apprehension, it went fine. Here are some things I suggest if you expect to meet his kids. (Since I don't have kids, I can't give you any suggestions for when he meets yours.)

💜 Make sure he knows the impact his comments about you can make to influence the kids' feelings toward you. He should be judicious — perhaps even guarded — about what he tells them about you. Of course, some of this has to do with their age, as younger kids may feel more threatened about you than older ones. And if his separation/divorce is recent, they may harbor hope that their parents will still reconcile so will resent you getting in the way.

💜 Ask him about their interests so you can ask

relevant questions. It helps break the ice if you can engage them about things that are important to them.

💜 Make sure he doesn't discuss your opinion of any challenges he faces with their behavior. That is between you and him. The kid may think you are trying to parent him/her, and if you are only dating it is too soon to step into this role.

💜 Bring a small gift you know s/he would enjoy on the first meeting. A book on a topic of interest, some favorite treat, a toy, etc. Nothing elaborate or it may feel like you're trying to buy the kid's affections.

💜 Avoid saying anything derogatory about your guy in front of the kid. Don't put Dad down even if you are kidding. It is okay to play around, but some children may take it out of context and feel you are putting down their beloved dad. Not a good way to start.

💜 Talk to your guy about doing something the kid(s) would like on a first outing. So don't go out to a white-tablecloth restaurant if the kid would rather go to Chili's. The first meeting should be as comfortable as possible for the child, no matter how old.

What have you found works when you meet your guy's kids for the first time?

Do you love how he loves you?

Do you know how you want to be loved? What if a man loves you, but not quite the way you want to be loved? Will you stick with him, thinking that you can teach him how you want to be loved? Has that worked?

I've been fortunate enough in my 3.5 years of dating to have a few men fall for me. While I was fond of them and loved elements of each one, I was not in love. As that old adage goes, "Love is not enough." We know that can mean lots of things, but let's take just one element — being loved is not enough. You have to feel loved — loved in a way that feels like love to you. How someone expresses his love for you may not feel like love to you. I know, this seems convoluted.

Let me elaborate.

Early in my marriage, my hubby and I would design quarterly relationship retreats — just him and me. We'd drive to a hotel for the weekend, and the activities included working on our relationship. (Too bad we didn't keep up this practice for the next 20 years!) One of the most memorable exercises was this simple one. We each silently wrote our responses to these two questions:

1. Here's what I do that I believe shows my love for you

2. Here's what you do that I feel shows your love for me

After writing our responses, we shared. The answers were astonishing to each of us.

My answer to question 1 included:

I take care of our bill paying

I prepare home-cooked meals that I know you like

I have your vodka and tonic chilled and waiting for you when you arrive home

It turns out none of these things — and many of the others I listed — were significant to him. So I was busting my tush to go out of my way to do these things to show him I loved him, and they didn't show up as love at all to him!

On his list of how he felt I showed him I loved him was one I would have never guessed:

You come out of your office and give me a hug soon after I announce I'm home.

I worked from home, so I was often in my office when he arrived home. I'd just call out "hello" in response to his "I'm home." It turned out that he wanted a physical connection — a hug and kiss — when he arrived home. He was a kinesthetic type and touch was very important to him to feel connected. When I learned this, I nearly always made sure to hug him hello. If I was on the phone when he came in and forgot to hug him, we noticed we were more on edge with each other that evening.

When he learned that his periodic gift of flowers felt like love to me, he increased his frequency. He also asked about my favorite flowers and began to select dual-toned, unusual ones, rather than just daisies, carnations and red roses. I was feeling more loved as he was going out of his way to learn what I liked and give it to me.

This exercise taught us to talk about what the other did that felt like love.

This exercise taught us to talk about what the other did that felt like love. And it allowed us to see if what we were doing was showing up as an expression of love to the other. And when it didn't, we could ditch it or do it if we wanted, but not expect the other would feel warm and tingly because of it. It also headed off those resentful arguments, like, "But I spend hours fixing dinner for you each night" when the other would just as soon open a can of soup or have take out.

It would be great if the guy you're dating intuitively knew how you like to be loved, but the recipe for each person is different. For some women, regular calls, sweet emails, occasional flowers and cards signify love. For others, none of that is important. The key is to know what exemplifies love to you and be willing to do the exercise above when you've been dating a guy for a while. You will both clarify how to show the other you care and refine your love strategies.

And of course, be appreciative of whatever he does to show his fondness toward you. Also, both parties need to be open to refinements.

The deliciousness of pillow talk

There's something delicious about late-night calls with your sweetheart. They are even more yummy than a mint on your pillow, and I love chocolate!

When snuggled in bed talking on the phone the conversation seems to get deeper, more tender, and of course, sometimes provocative! This virtual tucking in can bring you closer as long as one of you doesn't drift off. It seems easier to talk about hopes, dreams, fears and feelings than conversations in the light of day.

This virtual tucking in can bring you closer

Of course, I think the best time to discuss these things is when you are nestled in each others' arms. But absent the other's presence, you can envelope yourself in your sweetie's voice and words. You can really focus on what's being said without visual and tactile distractions.

This connectedness can help you drift to slumber-land feeling warm and loved. You'll likely have sweet dreams, a restful night and wake up refreshed — assuming you didn't talk 'til the wee hours! And when next you see your love, you'll feel closer.

How are you about receiving gifts from your guy?

Prior to my birthday, my beau at the time told me he'd been shopping for my gift. I'd forgotten to tell him that his presence was my present as he was already spending a lot on air fare. But he wanted to give me something I could hold — besides him!

The other reason I wanted to dissuade him from gift giving — but it was too late — is I'm hard to buy for. Dates and beaus have given me "safe" gifts of flowers, books, stuffed animals, etc. I appreciated their thoughtfulness even if I wasn't always thrilled with the gift itself. But I still liked how generous the guy was to not only think of giving me a gift, but to follow through.

Gift giving was usually traumatic in my childhood and marriage, so I still have some baggage around it. While I try to be Zen about it now and appreciate whatever I get — or nothing — it can still be a sore spot.

My ex's first gift was a tiny pendant he'd bought on a business trip a few months after we began dating. I'm a tall woman, 5'10" and not waif like, but not zaftig. I wear large earrings and necklaces to match my frame. This pendant would be like an ant on me — completely unnoticeable. I thanked him and put it in my jewelry box to remind me of his thinking of me, but I never wore it.

I enter this gift-receiving arena with trepidation

So you see, I enter this gift-receiving arena with trepidation.

Of course, I don't think I'm hard to buy for! (Do we ever see that in ourselves?) Only after my ex and I had many discussions about it did I come to see that my taste was challenging for him. My point of view was, "It would be easy if he just opened his eyes and looked and listened!" Hints were all around him. I am a fan of our local professional football team. Did he ever buy us tickets to a game? No, he bought me a life-sized cardboard cutout of my team's quarterback. I collect colored depression glass. Might he have gone to an antique store or eBay and rounded out my collection? No. I frequently play my favorite recording artists. Did I ever get one of their latest CDs? Never. If he'd just opened his eyes, he would have noticed I wear larger jewelry, not ant-sized pendants.

My question to you is, how are you when a beau gives you a gift for a significant occasion? Even if you graciously receive it in the moment, if it isn't on target, do you let him know? And what do you do then — stuff it in the closet, take it back, or re-gift it? If he's around your place much, he'll notice it isn't prominently displayed, used or worn. Then what?

And if this mis-gifting happens repeatedly, do you do what I've done in the past and make it mean that he isn't paying attention to you? Or do you just accept whatever is given as a token of his affection?

(And, dear readers, Godiva is always appreciated, even as a belated birthday gift. I'll gladly email my address to anyone who wants to send along a pound or two. <g>)

Slow down, you move too fast

I knew a colleague had been online dating so was interested in an update.

He had decided to run his dating life similarly to how he runs his business. He'd troll for suitable prospects on dating sites, then send an email to each with a link to a 12-page web site outlining every detail of who he is and who he is looking for. This page included much more information than an online profile allowed. In addition to his hobbies, profession, health, food, religion, he included his sexual frequency preference! He says this detailed information eliminated women who aren't a match.

A woman responded with a 3.5-page version of her own preferences in his categories. They met within days and she removed her profile within a week of posting it. Although they live a three-hour drive apart, after a few months dating, they are now engaged.

The missing piece of this story is that this 50-year-old colleague has been married four times before. I have no idea how long he dated before marrying, nor how long he was married to each. But based on this whirlwind romance, I'm wondering if he's repeating a pattern of quickly falling in love, marrying, then finding out what each other is really like, thus divorcing.

A nearly 60-year-old gal pal has been married five times. Again, I don't know how long the courtships or marriages lasted. Her last union was a few years. One could theorize that the marriages ended because they really didn't know each other and took the plunge too quickly.

In dating, when you meet someone who seems a great match, it's easy to fall quickly. And it's easy to ignore the wisdom that you would share with another who was making wedding plans within months of meeting: "Slow down!" When it is you, you argue, "But this is different" or "But he's The One" or "But I've never felt this way before." So why rush? If he's the one, he'll still be the one in 6 or 12 or 24 months, won't he? Why sprint to the altar?

When it is you, you argue, "But this is different"

You've heard of hasty marriages lasting a lifetime. But more frequently quickie nuptials crash and burn fast. Remember the hours-long Britney Spears marriage? You want to make sure it is likely to last before tying the knot. Divorces are just too damaging it's best to avoid them.

When you find yourself talking about moving in together or marriage within weeks of meeting someone, remember to recite the first line of Simon and Garfunkle's "The 59th Street Bridge Song (Feelin' Groovy)": "Slow down, you move too fast." But instead of "You've got to make the morning last" how about saying "We've got to make sure it will last."

Make sure to download your free eBook Attract Your Next Great Mate: Dating Advice From Top Relationship Experts at www.Dating-Goddess.com/freebie

Eliciting your friends' reactions to your guy

After dating a guy a while, you want to introduce him to your friends. You're hoping they'll see how terrific he is. But what if they don't? You are torn between wanting to know what they think ... and not. Some women defend their man if their friends

> *What if they see something glaring that you're overlooking?*

say anything negative about him. But what if they see something glaring that you're overlooking?

What if you could get their feedback in a non-threatening manner? Leslie, a friend of a friend, figured out a fun way to do this. She invited her close pals to a party to meet her new guy. Each guest was given a "Rate This Man!" card. After interacting with her new guy, before they left they marked their responses to multiple-choice questions:

First Impression

___ Not the pick of the litter. Good luck. No!

___ Could be a date. Will you share? Maybe.

___ He's a treasure. Yes!

Attractiveness

___ Keep the lights off; yikes! No!

___ OK, but I'd keep looking. Maybe.

___ Um, sorry, I got distracted. Yes!

Personality

___ A cold fish, throw him back. No!

___ Invite friends for company. Maybe.

___ A woman's man. Mmmmm. Yes!

Sexual Potential

___ Buy more batteries. No!

___ Oh, what the hell. It's only sex. Maybe.

___ I'm imagining …, yum. Yes!

Rate This Couple

___ Coffee shop only.

___ Could be fun.

___ Tropical honeymoon.

I wasn't at the event, nor do I know Leslie, but I'm imagining the guy in question was in on it from the beginning, perhaps even helping create the possible responses. If so, it would show he had a good sense of humor, was confident he'd get good scores, and was a good sport.

Did Leslie and Mr. X review the responses after everyone left? Imagine how awkward it would be if the majority of answers were in the "no" category. At minimum, it would be interesting conversation fodder. It would let you see how he reacted to the information — whether he took it good-naturedly, got defensive, or got angry. And it would give you a glimpse into what your friends thought, even though they may be less than candid.

Does it really matter what your friends think as long as you think he's great? Yes and no. If they are true friends, they are interested in your happiness and good will. Their antennae will be looking for any yellow flags that you may have overlooked. But most friends won't offer this feedback freely, unless you have asked and they believe you really want it.

Everyone's opinion is filtered through their own biases. Mr. X may have reminded your best friend of her ex, so she hated him immediately. A male buddy may be harboring a crush on you, so will only point out the negatives of your new guy. Or your sister longs for a relationship so much and so wishes one for you that she'd give thumbs up to any man with a job who's breathing.

And yet you have to balance their opinions with

how you feel. After all, you're the one dating him and hanging out with him. You may see a tender, caring, sensitive side that doesn't come out in a party situation.

So if you hear a trend in your friends' comments, take it to heart. But if only one person doesn't like him, chalk it up to his/her bias. Ideally, you're able to keep a fair and balanced view of your guy, even as you're falling for him.

Favors during dating — good or bad idea?

"Women grow attached to men through the favors they grant them; but men, through the same favors, are cured of their love." —Jean de la Bruyere

This quote made me examine my attitude about favors, as hopefully it will you, too.

Do you grow fond of men by the things they do for you? Holding doors, taking you out, doing small chores around your home? I know I do. When a man goes out of his way to do things for me, it makes me feel closer to him. Some men seem to revel in doing "boyfriend jobs," often without asking, and especially if they are acknowledged for it.

I never thought that men may react unfavorably to my doing favors for them. I did a lot of favors for my ex … hmmm, maybe that's part of why he's my ex!

Some men seem to revel in doing "boyfriend jobs"

But men I've dated seemed to appreciate when I cooked them a meal or did little things for them. But then, none of them are around anymore, so maybe they were "cured of their love." I find it hard to imagine that men don't like their women doing nice things for them, but I can also see that they could feel smothered or that the woman appears too needy.

What do you think about giving and receiving favors to/from the person you're dating? Is this another example of Mars/Venus where men and women react differently?

Have you watched your sweetie at work?

Wen a man greets you for the first time with "My, my, my," you know it's going to be a good date!

Thus began my dinner date with a guy we'll call Mr. Radio Guy since he is the headliner DJ at a R&B station. Even before meeting him, we clicked with our love of R&B. Our online and voice chats were fun, flirty and interesting. He sent me a recording of him on the air since his station is out of state. He's moving to my area in a few weeks and was in town to make final arrangements with his new station.

Yes, he has those dulcet tones discussed "Are you drawn to deep-voiced men?" (in the *In Search of King Charming: Who Do I Want to Share My Throne?* book). It is fun to re-listen to his recording. I realized very few of us get to experience our sweeties at work, watching them perform their jobs superbly. He promised I will have ample opportunity to hear him on the air, as well as watch as he emcees concerts with recording stars (and get back-stage passes, too!).

There is something magical about watching — or listening — to someone with whom you are fond doing a stellar job. My ex was a storyteller, so I regularly watched him perform and beamed as he spun his tales. Then when he became a minister, I enjoyed watching him deliver his sermons (many of which I co-wrote). You see the person in a different light, appreciating a talent you might not have seen before. I delight in watching collegial friends deliver a home-run presentation.

However, when the roles are reversed I find myself a little nervous. When someone I am sweet on sits in my presentation, I'm a tad self-conscious, concerned that he may notice my mistakes. When my ex and I would co-present, we would make notes for each other on what could be improved. While this was helpful, it was also a bit nerve-wracking. It is usually easy to identify the things you know you screwed up, and it is hard to hear someone else point them out.

One of the keys to having this go well is to make sure you only comment on what you liked, and reserve any suggestions to when — and if — he asks. If he feels you are criticizing him, you'll never be invited to watch again. So even if you see something egregious, bite your tongue unless he specifically asks for any improvement ideas.

Have you had someone you're dating experience you at work? Maybe you've dated a colleague who attended meetings with you, or a customer? Or have you been able to experience someone you're dating doing his work? Did that shift your fondness of him?

Try a heart share

A common complaint from women is they can't get their guy to open up — to share his innermost thoughts, fears, and dreams. This is difficult to do for many people, women as well as men.

During my marriage, I learned a technique that made it easier to be vulnerable and talk about things that you might not normally discuss. We learned it from our relationship counselor, a gifted woman named Sonika Tinker, MSW.

Before I share the technique, let me tell you why we went to Sonika. When we were first married, we'd plan quarterly relationship retreats for ourselves. Since we were both seminar leaders, it was fun sharing the design of a special workshop just for us. We soon realized it was hard to be designer, facilitator and participant, so we sought someone else to lead us. That's when we found Sonika. We set up quarterly meetings with her to work on deepening our relationship and work out any kinks that we weren't comfortable bringing up on our own. I likened our relationship to a high performing car needing frequent tune ups to continue to run well. (I was delusional about lots of things in my marriage!)

Sonika suggested we do what she dubbed "heart shares" at least once a week, right before lights out when we were still lucid enough to be fully present. So not lying in bed before drifting to sleep. But going to bed half-hour early, lighting some candles and snuggling. A heart share isn't reporting what happened during the day, or what you have coming up tomorrow. It has nothing to do with tasks.

Instead, it is being vulnerable to your partner, sharing concerns you have about your life, health, or loved ones. Or it could be sharing a dream for the future in a way that in another setting you may withhold because you're concerned your partner may think it's silly or be threatened (if it's a direction different than you know s/he wants to go).

It is being vulnerable to your partner

The key when you are listening to a heart share is to really work at active listening. You're saying, "Shouldn't you do that all the time?" But we don't when we're talking about the mundane logistics of life. So when you're listening to your partner, work to listen without interrupting, breathe in tandem, show you're listening, not redirect the conversation to what you want, or object to what's being said. If he raises a doubt or concern, you can say, "I can understand how you might feel that way,"

but you aren't — at that moment — to tell him why his perception is wrong.

Each person gets 10-15 minutes. When it feels one is winding up, the listener says, "Is there anything else?" You want the other to feel complete. Then you switch.

When both of you are done, you may want to go back and say, "Wow. I never realized you had a dream of being a citizen of the world. Have you thought of how we could make that happen, even on a small scale at first?" Or, "I understand your feelings of inadequacy about creating a loving committed relationship since your ex cheated on you." You're not problem solving here. You're just showing you listened, and wanting more information if needed.

Heart shares don't have to wait until a couple is in a committed relationship. They can happen when you feel safe and connected enough to allow yourself to be vulnerable without fear of being chastised or ridiculed. At first they may seem awkward. But if both of you want to have a deeper emotional connection, you can introduce this topic and approach the first few as practice, knowing that you will have some kinks to work out.

The downsides of always getting your way

mature, sane man who's interested in wooing you generally wants to make you happy. But how can always getting what you want make you unhappy? A fellow strong woman and I were discussing this recently.

> *"While I appreciate that my man is interested in making me happy, sometimes it can be a weight," she shared.*

> *"In what way?" I queried.*

> *"If he's not willing to speak up about what he wants, then I feel I need to take into consideration what I think he would like before deciding something. So if he asks me what movie I want to see, I could choose a chick flick, but know he wouldn't be thrilled. So I choose one that may not be at the top of my list, but know he's more likely to enjoy."*

> *That just seems considerate. Why is that a problem?"*

"*Because I'm not then being exposed to movies that he might suggest and I wouldn't have thought of. Instead of broadening my options, I'm limited to only what I think of or know about.*

"*Also, a relationship should be 50/50. I want to give him what he wants equally. By his not thinking about what he wants and sharing it, I'm not really getting to know his true desires. If he constantly puts my preferences above his, he's hiding from me.*"

"*I can see that. Also, I've found when someone acquiesces too much, it is tedious to always make the decisions. I used to ski with a woman who would never make a decision about which runs we should take. 'Whatever you want,' she'd say. I noticed how much work it was to decide the runs I knew she could handle. Finally, I said, 'You pick the runs in the morning and I'll choose them for the afternoon.' It felt much more balanced that way.*"

"*Yes, you're then not feeling responsible for them.*"

"*Exactly.*"

What downsides have you found to always getting your way?

Giving and receiving emotional support

"My ex-girlfriend wanted me to support her emotionally, but she didn't do the same in return," my date shared.

"Hmm. I'm not sure I'd know the signs that someone was wanting emotional support unless they were crying or upset. What are the signs you want or need emotional support?" I asked.

"Good question. I don't really know. I just know I didn't get what I needed from her when I had an upsetting day."

"What was missing that you wanted? If I were to emotionally support you, what would that look like?"

"Again, a great question. I'm not sure."

So he didn't know how to tell he needed it, or what it would look like, but he knew he didn't get it. Sounds a bit convoluted, but I think we can relate to knowing something is missing, but not knowing exactly what that is. For some, it would be a lack of compliments or positive acknowledgment of your accomplishments. For others it is listening when one had an upsetting event or a bad day, without the other offering solutions.

Being a bit unsure myself of what emotional support meant exactly, I asked a very emotionally supportive friend for her definition.

> *"When someone is upset, you don't try to solve the problem, especially since some are without resolution, especially around kids or spouses. But instead, just to actively listen, and ask about the person's feelings. Things like, 'How did that make you feel?' or 'I bet that hurt your feelings,' or 'Why do you think that comment hit you so hard?' You don't focus on activities, outcomes or solutions, but instead on helping them identify their feelings, and then, if they are interested, on the source of those feelings."*

When I've been upset and someone has commented on my emotions, I've felt absolutely heard. If someone focuses on just the solution I feel less heard. We know this intellectually, and many of us have taken (or taught!) courses on active listening, but sometimes in our romantic relationships we forget to apply what we know.

If someone focuses on just the solution I feel less heard

How do you let someone know you need emotional support? Early in my marriage, I tried to offer suggestions to ease my ex's upsets. (I know this is counter-stereotypical.) He finally told me he needed me to hear him out first, before offering solutions. For a while after that I'd ask, "Do you want me in active-listening mode or in problem-solving mode?" Nearly always he'd say the former. I learned to listen first and he'd let me know when he wanted some ideas for solutions.

Do you know how to let someone else know you need emotional support? And what exactly it looks like to you — active listening, being held, only asking questions, not offering solutions? And do you know how to detect when your guy wants emotional support? What does it look like to him? It may be very different than what you need.

Is it persuasion, manipulation or enticement?

Persuasion: *a means of persuading someone to do something*

Manipulate: *control or influence (a person or situation) cleverly, unfairly, or unscrupulously*

Entice: *attract or tempt by offering pleasure or advantage*

Recently I was accused of trying to manipulate someone. It threw me for a loop as that was 180% opposite of my intention. I wasn't even trying to persuade nor entice them. An off-hand comment that I thought was being playful was taken in the worst possible way and elicited an indictment of my morals, integrity and motives. I was quite taken aback.

It caused me to examine the word and the distinction between persuasion, manipulation and enticement, especially in the context of dating and romantic relationships.

I know certain words, phrases and images are enticing to many men. When in a healthy relationship, you learn what your man wants and work to give it to him. Is that manipulative? Only if you want something in return other than his happiness. Of course, if he is happy, he will be more compelled to make you happy. So by giving him what he wants are you being manipulative? Or just enticing?

A gal pal knows her husband likes to have sex every three days. She says she makes sure to oblige, as he is much more receptive then to doing the things she wants. Is she being manipulative? Persuasive? Enticing? Or is she just giving him what she knows he wants?

By midlife, most of us know how to tell a man what we want and how to acknowledge him when he gives it to us. We know he wants to make us happy. For many men, making us happy is a primary goal. However, what if he knows that if he makes us happy outside the bedroom, we will be more enthusiastic about having sex with him? So this is the other side of the scenario in the previous paragraph. What if my friend's husband did what she wanted knowing she'd be more prone to have sex more frequently?

What do you think about giving your sweetheart what you know he wants? Are you just being smart, working to have a happy man and relationship, or is there some manipulation involved?

Is he collecting data on how to make you happy?

I briefly dated a man who interspersed into our conversations a myriad of questions about my preferences. He asked about my favorite flower, gemstone, color, fabric, musical artist, book genre, movie type, restaurants, foods, thing to do on a sunny day, coffee shop, travel destinations, pet peeves, etc. After a few questions, I asked why he wanted to know. "I'm noting them for future reference. I want to make you happy, so need to know what will do so."

Wow! No one else has been as overt in his probing for my happiness makers. I was impressed with his diligence. The connection fizzled before he had a chance to deliver on any of this knowledge. But the fact that he was gathering it was a sign that he knew what information to gather and seemed — at least initially — to care about making me happy.

Could he have intended to use this information to manipulate me? Perhaps. But since I'm an interpret-things-positively kinda gal, I wouldn't assume that unless I saw evidence to support that negative interpretation.

Of course, happiness does not revolve around receiving a favorite flower. It's more important how a man speaks to you, is respectful, keeps his word, listens and generally treats you well. But if all the right behaviors are in place, it's added enhancement if he 1) cares enough to know what you like, and 2) provides those things regularly, willingly, and with love. A smart man understands this is part of the ongoing romancing of his sweetie.

Do you collect info on your guy's favorites? I am less apt to be as overt as the man described above, but I do make note of how he takes his coffee, what he regularly drinks, teams he roots for, etc. If I'm seeing two guys concurrently, I'll make a note about this information in each man's file in my Date-A-Base (see the *Multidating Responsibly: Play the Field Without Being A Player* book). (It's too much to remember about multiple men.)

How would you like it if a man was methodical about collecting your preferences? Would you like it or think it was a tad creepy? And how do you go about noting what your guy likes?

Does "settling down" mean "settling"?

"You've dated a lot of men now. You've been seeing a terrific guy. Why don't you just decide to focus on him and settle down?" My friend was concerned with my playing the field and thought I would be better off just choosing one man on whom to focus.

"But if I know he's not yet lighting my fire, aren't I set-tling? I want to be excited by my man. I like this man a lot; we have a lot in common. I'm glad when I know I'm going to see him, but not excited."

> If I know he's not yet lighting my fire, aren't I settling?

"Then why do you still see him?"

"I'm testing the theory that you can become more excited about a guy after you get to know him well.

Some say it's true. I haven't experienced that before. He's too good a guy to not at least give it a try.

"We have both stated that we're not yet in love. We are building a foundation of friendship. So I wonder at what point do we say, 'We gave it a good run. We're both very fond of each other. But neither of us has fallen in love. So we should declare we are really good friend material.'"

"I just hate to see you go up and down the emotional roller coaster. It must be exhausting."

"Actually, it can be occasionally, but generally the roller coaster is pretty sedate. Once in a great while I'll get my hopes up then watch them get dashed. But luckily that's pretty few and far between. I guess I'm becoming a better man picker, even if I haven't figured out the formula for a picking a great guy for me. At least I don't find myself with many drama kings."

So what do you think about settling down with — and settling for — someone who doesn't excite you but has many, many, many wonderful qualities? Would you give it a go and see if you could find a way to get your motor revving when with him? We know that too much sexual energy can mask glaring personality flaws. What about medium energy on your side, but high on his?

Falling in …????

Y ou've begun to date a guy you like. Each encounter makes you like him more. He's funny, thoughtful, smart, romantic. He cares about making you happy. He's not self-absorbed. He sends you sweet, caring emails and gives you sincere compliments. You find yourself falling in…??? What? What is this?

Like? Are you falling in like? You definitely like him. But it sounds so platonic. So high school. So insufficient for your affection toward him. But yet you know that it is important — nay, critical — to like someone with whom you want to spend more time. In fact, there may be people in your life (e.g., relatives) who you love but don't really like. You don't relish spending time with them. But you know they love you and you love them.

Are you falling in fond? This is not a term we hear. But you are definitely fond of him. You grow fonder all the time. He hasn't dipped into the disappointment side of the Delight/Disappointment Scale (in the *Real Deal or Faux Beau: Should You Keep Seeing Him?* book) — or at least rarely. He's brought you flowers, showered you with affection, and an appropriate amount of calls and emails to tell you he cares about you and misses you.

He takes you on fun outings and always seems happy to talk and be with you.

Or is it lust? Maybe he has heavenly kisses, delicious caresses, and even holding hands gives you goose bumps. You are definitely hot for each other. Maybe you have — or haven't — slept together, but either way there is definitely sexual appeal. Maybe you've fallen in lust. (See "Falling in lust," page 131.)

Or are you falling in love? Love is such a nebulous term. I wish there were as many words to describe the gradations of fondness, adoration and endearment as there were Inuit/Eskimo words for snow. Yes, you love him — you love the way he makes you laugh, his tenderness, his willingness to talk about important things, his awareness when he's done something wrong, his insatiable appetite for self-improvement — and dark chocolate. You love many things about him. So are you in love?

Love is such a nebulous term

Whatever you call it, you're enjoying it. So continue to bask in it and see if you can avoid labeling it as long as possible. There are some drawbacks to labels.

A downside to labeling it "falling in love" too soon

is that you may not really know the person yet. After a few dates, I was obviously acting love-struck when a guy asked, "Are you falling in love with me?" I was surprised by the question, and uttered, "I'm moving in that direction." It was folly as I barely knew him. I liked how he'd treated me so far, but after a few more dates I discovered a mean streak that hadn't surfaced. I'd let myself think I was falling for a guy I hardly knew.

Another possible downside is you may feel embarrassed a few weeks later when you have to explain to your friends why you're no longer together. They may ask, "I thought you were in love?" To which you may have to respond, "I thought I was, too." Your judgment will be questioned and the next time you declare yourself in love they will roll their eyes.

Or maybe it will be scary for him if you tell him you're falling in love and he'll back off. Some men get afraid that you are expecting a commitment if you tell them you're falling in love. You will only see a flash as he mumbles, "Exit, stage left."

So wait a little while before you declare you are in love, and instead be happy to be in like, fond, or even lust.

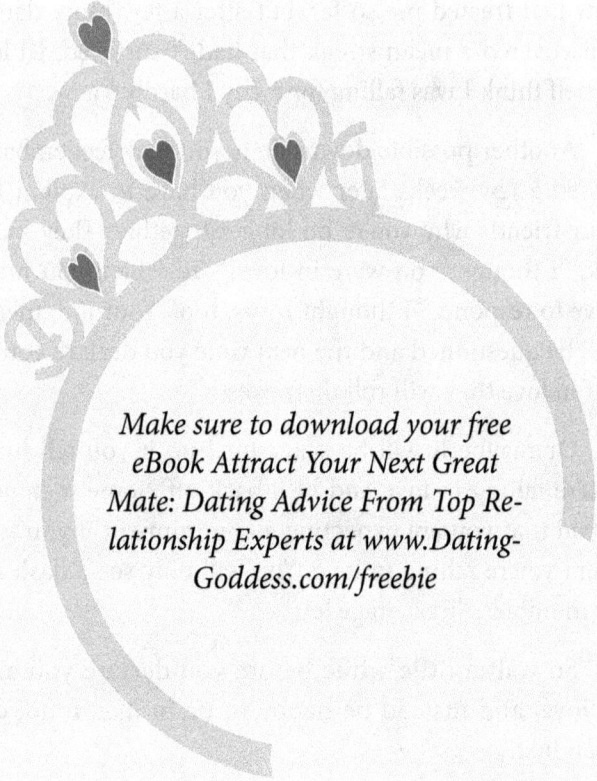

*Make sure to download your free
eBook Attract Your Next Great
Mate: Dating Advice From Top Relationship Experts at www.Dating-
Goddess.com/freebie*

Be careful of being smitten

As I was enthusiastically describing to a friend my fondness for my newest gentleman caller, she asked, "Are you smitten?" I pondered, then replied, "No, enamored." We then discussed the difference.

The dictionary describes smitten as, "To affect sharply with great feeling; marked by foolish or unreasoning fondness." Enamored: "To inspire with love; captivate."

"Smitten" seems school-girlish, a giggly crush

"Smitten" seems school-girlish, a giggly crush; all reasonableness vanishes. When I'm smitten I ignore glaring red flags that say, "This is not a good match." Thinking back on my smitten experiences, none of them have been good choices, but something strong pulled me in. When you are smitten, you put your good sense on the back burner and do spontaneous — and sometimes stupid — things.

"Enamored" feels more grounded, more mature, longer lasting. I still think about him throughout the day, look forward to our talks. I'm strongly fond of him. But I also know his foibles and have decided they aren't deal breakers.

So if you find yourself caught up quickly in romance, feeling swept away, intoxicated, and hearing yourself say, "I've never done this/felt this way before," enjoy the spontaneity and excitement, but put the brakes on before you do something you'll regret.

Becoming besotted

Are you easily beguiled? Do you wear your heart on your sleeve? Are you prone to become prematurely smitten?

Or are you more cautious, perhaps bordering on detached, especially early on in dating someone? You keep your heart sheltered for as long as possible? Then you either succumb to being moonstruck or lose interest as there's no heart connection?

I work to strike a balance knowing that most people are on their best behavior in the first few dates so I like to be a balance of engaged and detached. But once in a great while I'll meet a guy who I go over the moon for quickly. Wham! He seems like the real deal. But so far, those have rarely lasted a month. The love-comet burns out quickly.

A month of dating seems to be a watershed for me. If we can both be infatuated after seeing each other a month, it says a lot. "A month?" you may be saying. "That's no time at all."

You'd be right. You have barely scratched the surface, no matter how many dates, calls, and IMs you've had. No matter how many marathon dates you've been on, and how much sharing you have done.

It's been a month since I began seeing a man I like a lot. So far, he has not slackened his pace in sending daily multiple romantic texts, calling regularly, and generally being someone I'm drawn to. Is he perfect? No, but if his imperfection gets in the way of our connecting, I let him know how I feel. So far he seems perfect for me. I know I have glaring imperfections, but he's not mentioned any to me. Perhaps he has more grace than me!

When I think of the many qualities I adore about him, I see that he personifies many of the characteristics I've longed for in a man. I admit that I've been treated well by a few men in the past, but I never grew to love them as they did me. I realize that sounds arrogant and egotistical, so forgive me. But the contrast of the past — either of my being smitten or the guy being beguiled — is that this time it appears we are mutually infatuated.

The question remains, can this intensity last beyond the next month or so? I'd like to think it can. I know our irritants will surface and it will tell a lot how we chose to deal with them.

What are the signs you've noticed that told you that besottedness will continue beyond the initial flush of adoration?

Falling in lust

"Too much of a good thing can be wonderful."
—Mae West

How do you know you're falling in love vs. falling in lust? I don't have the answer — I'm hoping you do! All I know is it feels like I'm falling in something!

Here's what's happening:

I met an amazing guy. Everything clicked. I mean everything. There were no red flags — is that a red flag that he has no immediately detectible flaws?

> *Is it a red flag that he has no immediately detectible flaws?*

We spent a lot of time together the next evening. Still, no glaring character flaws. No obnoxious habits so far. I know, you're saying, "You've only just begun to know him so he's on his best behavior. The flaws will come out." But usually when I've spent this amount of time with someone, their quirks have begun to show.

The confusion about lust vs. love comes when he's

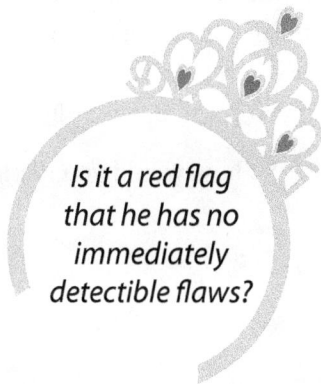

got the important items on your "perfect man" list (tall, good looking, fit, funny, intelligent, thoughtful, chivalrous, educated, articulate) and there's physical magnetism (love his energy, his kisses, his tender caresses). So are these all components of love, or does chemistry (lust) take over? Or is lust just a key factor in falling in love?

One guy pal described the difference:"When it's lustful you think about touching her breasts. When it's love you think about holding hands when older." We decided love is when you want both.

I've fallen in lust before. You have barely met yet can't keep your hands off each other. Things progress quickly, and soon you're intertwined. After a few encounters, you realize you don't really know the person. One of you steps back and says, "We need to slow down." Or you realize you're further along than you want to be, so you break up — or just vanish.

So how would you distinguish the two?

Exclusivity: How and when to broach it

An Adventures in Delicious Dating After 40 reader wrote:

> How and when do you decide to date just one person? I struggle with this issue. I figure I'll wait 'til they bring it up, but they haven't, and I'm pretty sure they've assumed we're an item and I'm not dating others. Although I prefer to keep my options open and date more than one until we have an agreement, I think I risk alienating really great guys who might be surprised and dismayed to find I'm open to dating others. And yet, I do like to keep a full social schedule. Such a predicament.
>
> I seem to have a high capacity for socializing at this time in my life, and am looking for a guy who ultimately wants to be together maybe four or even five nights a week. Perhaps that's higher than average? Just like I wanted, I'm finding wonderful, balanced men who have friends and outside

activities. However, they don't seem to have the same dating capacity I do. So although I want an exclusive relationship, I feel that rather than have unrealistic expectations of them or (worse!) compromise what I want, perhaps I should just continue the odd additional date here and there to keep my schedule as full as I like. Really, two men would be perfect, and I even have the 2 lined up, but would they go for that? And would dating two 'exclusively' jeopardize both? Should I just do it and not bring it up?

The "experts" say to let the guy bring up exclusivity, otherwise you'll sound needy. I've recommended this myself.

The one time I've brought up the topic, it turned out I was more into him than he me. So while he agreed to exclusivity, he never provided what I neded in the relationship.

The "experts" say to let the guy bring up exclusivity

The reason I've not brought it up with others is even if I dated a guy for a while I wasn't convinced we were long-term material. So not bringing it up allowed me to still date around with impunity.

At this point, I've decided it depends on how in-

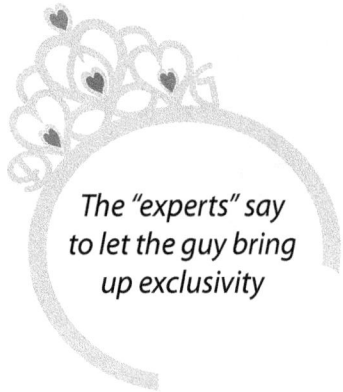

terested I am with focusing on just the beau du jour. It there isn't anyone that pulls your attention away from him, and you think you are pretty well suited, why not focus on just him and see how it plays out?

However, if you don't think he can fill your needs, why settle on just one? But maybe he doesn't realize you'd like to have more together time, so I'm all for bringing it up. While these conversations are difficult to begin, they are so much better than assuming. Perhaps he is willing to see you 3-4 days a week. Then you can tell him your other options are to see other guys or go out with gal pals. See what he says. If he says, "Go ahead and see other guys," you know he's not serious about you, and if that's okay with you, great. You can still play together when it fits your calendars, but he may also be playing with other women.

But if you've dated him multiple times and don't say anything about seeing others, I think you are setting yourself up for some drama. Best to put the cards on the table and if the chips fly, so be it (sorry for the poker metaphor!).

For me, I'm leaning toward having the exclusivity discussion as you get nearer having sex together. At that point, I think it appropriate to ask how the other feels about dating others and share your truthful opinion. I think he will get it if you couch it like, "I don't think you'd like it if I was sleeping with other men, and so I don't want you sleeping with other women while we're being intimate. While I'm not asking for or expecting a long-term commitment, I am asking for and expecting we both won't see others while we are seeing each other." Then ask what he thinks about this.

You'll find out very soon how he feels — assuming he is honest.

And no, girlfriend, you cannot date two men "exclusively!"

Let us know what you do and how it turns out!

Becoming a "boo"

What is a boo? Does it have something to do with ghosts? When doubled, does it refer to a child's scraped knee?

No. It is from the language of the street, sometimes referred to as "ghetto" or "urban."

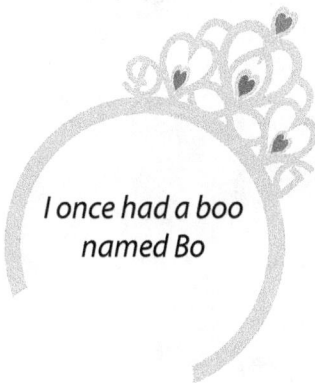

A "boo" is a beau, sweetheart, boyfriend/girlfriend, main squeeze. (I once had a boo named Bo.) You've moved from "we're talkin'," to "kinda be likin'," to "going out," to boo.

I once had a boo named Bo

What is involved in being a boo? Being exclusive, of course. Talking at least once a day, seeing each other regularly, becoming a part of each other's lives. No different than what you think of with the other terms, just a hipper name.

The journey of my becoming a boo began in one of our early conversations. We were IMing and somehow a comment about "street" language came up. I said I knew a little "street," and used the example, "He's my boo." Raucous laughter erupted at the receiving end of the message as my boo-to-be took a long break from the keyboard to roll on the floor. I had no idea this would be the response, but I guess the image of a 52-year-old white woman uttering this was just too much. He said he fell for me right then.

Later, thinking of Beyoncé's "bootylicous" moniker, I dubbed myself "boolicious." It stuck. That's become my nickname with him. So he is Boo and I am Boolicious.

So next time you want to appear hip, try working "boo" into the conversation. However, if you're a middle-aged white person talking to those who know "street," prepare for peals of laughter.

The 60-day relationship review

Most companies require new employees to undergo a 30-, 60-, and/or 90-day review to discuss how they are doing at their job. Typically part of the discussion is how well the employee thinks s/he is doing and what s/he likes and doesn't like about the job. The boss then shares how she thinks the employee is doing, what is working and what needs improvement.

I think relationships should have a 60-day (or 90-day) relationship review. This way both parties could get a reality check on how s/he sees the relationship in comparison to the other. Both people could answer the questions, first on paper, then sharing their answers with the other. Some sample questions could be:

> On a scale of 1-10, how well do you think the relationship is going, considering we've been seeing each other for two months?
>
> What do you feel is going well?
>
> What would you like more of?

What would you like less of?

What would it take for this relationship to be a 10 for you?

Do you think we should continue seeing each other?

You are not asking for a commitment, but honestly assessing and sharing how each other feels. If there is a big disparity — you rate the relationship an 8 and he gives it a 4 — then time to decide if the gap can be closed and what it would take to close it.

You may learn that what he needs for it to be a 7, 8, or 9 are things you can't provide. Maybe he wants to be with you five days a week and your schedule won't accommodate that.

Or maybe you'll discover other discrepancies. You can then discuss them and make a mature decision whether to continue seeing each other or not.

Some people don't want to have this discussion because they think it will upset the apple cart and drive the guy away. My attitude is if having a conversation like this after dating for two months would drive him away, then you're better off without him. The value of having this review is that you can see how you both feel. And if you need to move on, best to know now rather than waiting another two months.

What questions would you ask at the two-month mark?

Falling in love one drop at a time

Have you noticed that people fall in love with varying rapidity? For some, it's a wham, all-at-once thing soon — sometimes minutes — after meeting someone. For others, it may take years. For some it's a slow-but-steady thing, like coffee dripping through the filter one drop at a time. It's a thousand drops that bring you to the final brewed result — rich, full-flavored love.

Just as a cup of gourmet coffee consist of various beans, roasting methods, water, spices, etc., so too the heart-winning blend in your pot of love. Some components could include:

- the way he smiles
- how he looks at you
- how he dresses
- his laugh
- his kisses

- how he touches you
- little things he says that show he's thoughtful and caring
- how he stands and walks (posture)
- his thoughtfulness and respectfulness toward you and others
- how he makes you laugh
- his voice
- how he makes you feel special, feel loved
- his smell
- how he treats you generally
- flowers, cards, gifts or other ways he tangibly shows he cares
- his grooming that shows he takes pride in his presentation
- his self esteem
- his willingness to improve himself (going to the gym, classes, counseling)
- his values

Ways he tangibly shows he cares

💜 how he articulates his thoughts

💜 what he gives his time to

💜 what he does when I'm ill

💜 how seriously he takes me

💜 how he playfully teases me

💜 how I respect his decisions

💜 how he treats animals

💜 a spark in his eye

💜 how playful he is

💜 his idea of fun

💜 how he hugs me

What are other ingredients in your love blend? What makes you fall for a man?

When he tells you he loves you

You've been dating a guy for a little while — no more than a month. You get along great, enjoy your time together, and perhaps have had a sleepover. But you're just getting to know each other, and you aren't even sure if you're interested in him long-term, although you enjoy his company. But there are some yellow flags that make you doubt that you'll be together in six months. You try to put aside your concerns and just focus on enjoying your time together.

Then it happens. As he hugs and kisses you good-bye, he whispers in your ear, "I love you."

You freeze. While you've longed to hear those three words — but not necessarily from him — you are caught off guard. What do you do? Do you utter "I love you" back, even though you know you are fond of him, but don't quite feel "love" at this point? Or do you convince yourself that loving someone is the same as being fond of them, so it's okay to say it?

If you hesitate too long, he'll know it's an obligatory "I love you," not a heartfelt one. How do you respond — with "Thank you," "I know" or "There are many things I love about you, too"? These sound so flat. But if you say those three words and don't truly mean them, will more harm be done? So should you not say anything?

*The quandary is when you love him, but not **in love** with him*

The quandary is when you know you care for him, are fond of him, yes, perhaps even love him, but you know you're not *in* love with him. The former can be felt for anyone toward whom you have affection. The latter is for very few — someone who makes your heart beat faster, you ache for when he's away, have a mix of excitement and calm when you hear his voice, and get those silly goose bumps when he strokes your arm or kisses you. "In love" is reserved for someone with whom you think you could go the distance, will have your back, and be your partner, mate or husband.

So, what do you say when he says, "I love you" and you're not ready to say it back? Maybe you know you'll never be able to sincerely say "I'm in love with you," but right now you have to say something.

At this time, a simple whispered, "Thank you, sweetie" should suffice. But the next time you talk, you need to bring up how you feel. Something like, "I really appreciated your telling me you love me the other day. I like how you are able to express your feelings to me. I want you to know that I am very fond of you, and it takes me a while to feel I love someone. I don't want you to think I don't care about you if I don't say 'I love you.' And I don't want you to feel you can't say it to me if that's what you'd like to do."

But the larger picture needs to be addressed at some point. If you are both seeing this as an activity-partner-with-benefits relationship, then the "love" issue shouldn't be a problem. But when one of you sees the other as "The One" and the other realizes that s/he probably won't ever feel that way, it's best to get that out in the open. If it is you who is not feeling it, then it's your responsibility to start the conversation and be as gentle as possible. You don't want to lead him on if he has a different expectation.

However, I also know that this conversation can create hurt and upset, even if you've been honest all along that you're not "in love." False expectations can build up quickly. So it's best not to let the fantasies simmer.

What have you done when you've heard "I love you" before you're feeling it, or when you hear it and know you'll never feel similarly?

The power of appreciation in dating

Many years ago I heard a speaker state that 95% of communication in a romantic relationship should be acknowledgment. In other words, most of what you say to each other should be positive, complimentary and affirmative of the other.

This made me look at my own communication with my then husband. I didn't track the percentage of acknowledgment, but I'm sure it wasn't near 95%. Most of our communication was about daily tasks (what shall we have for dinner, who'll pick up the dry cleaning, updates to our personal calendars). There was some discussion about daily events and some about our relationship, people in our lives, and getting advice from the other. While we weren't nitpicky or regularly critical of each other, I noticed we weren't overly complimentary either.

Since I tended to voice my dissatisfaction more than him, I decided to step up my acknowledgment of him and reduce anything that could be construed critical. I'd save anything that he might feel was not positive to only the big things that were really important to me. I'd begin to shower him with compliments.

It was hard. Not that there weren't positive things to notice and comment on, but you have to train yourself to not just see something, but to say something.

And then how complimentary should one be about mundane things? Does it sound condescending when you say, "I'm glad you put on your seat belt,"

How complimentary should one be about mundane things?

"Thanks for taking out the trash," and "I appreciate it when you put your dirty clothes in the hamper"? When these are minimal co-living standards, should they be acknowledged? When I was a teenager, my mother complained that we never complimented her on dinner, so I suppose even agreed-upon chores still need acknowledgment.

My friend Mike Robbins is a master at how to verbally appreciate someone and have them hear it. He is the author of *Focus on the Good Stuff: The Power of Appreciation*. I invited Mike to present to 50 managers as part of a year-long management training program I was leading for a client. Within an hour, he had taught these managers the skills they needed to share sincere appreciation with each other, and to take these skills back to

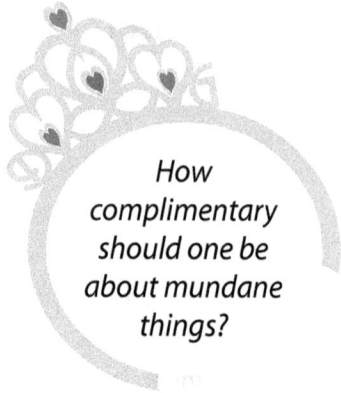

their departments. I watched seasoned managers get touched to tears hearing their colleagues' comments about how they made a difference in the other's life.

I've brought Mike's teachings to my dating adventure. I am more conscious of sharing my appreciation on a date, especially when I know he's gone out of his way for me. Mike teaches you to not just say, "Thank you for taking me to such a lovely restaurant." But to add, "I know you put effort in choosing a place you thought I'd enjoy. Your thoughtfulness makes me feel cared about and closer to you."

Granted, I am not the master at this that Mike is and I still have a ways to go in practicing this regularly. But when I have remembered to do this, I've seen my date not only smile, but stand up a bit taller and seem to beam a bit.

"Help your date notice his riches" (in the *First-Rate First Dates: Increasing the Chances of a Second Date* book) talked about commenting on things you think a date does well. Try coupling that with acknowledging how his behaviors make you feel good and see what happens.

Removing your mask

Most of us wear a mask, presenting ourselves as we want people to perceive us, not only in dating but in life. We decide how much and how soon to reveal our true selves based on the connection and trust we have with another. If we are feeling safe enough to let our hair down, we reveal our authentic selves, warts and all. Sometimes this occurs soon after beginning dating; other times it takes a while, depending on if we feel we'll still be loved no matter how odious we feel our real self is.

This mask can protect vulnerabilities about which you feel shame or embarrassment — behaviors you know aren't pretty. It can be withholding opinions or observations that you think the other won't take well, but they are part of your truth about him or the relationship. People can live with someone for years before letting their true self be seen. At that point, their mate may say, "This is not the person I married" and feel betrayed, duped, or happy with the person who has emerged.

With new relationships, we want our best self to appear. We know how to behave so he wants to hang around us (assuming we want to be around him!). But as you get to know each other, your guard is dropped and you start behaving less than perfectly. You feel it's okay, as you've learned to trust him and believe he will continue to be attracted to you.

How fast is too fast to remove this mask? How far is too far? As you remove your mask, you may cross a boundary that the other feels is unacceptable. You may reveal bitchiness, judmentalness, emotionality, or cynicism. Each couple has to learn each person's boundaries and know how to communicate calmly and kindly when the boundary is crossed.

Much of how the communication will be received is in timing and voice tone. While you may feel you are being clear, he feels patronized. He thinks he's just being direct and you feel chastised. As absurd as it might sound, you may want to set up some ground rules — or boundaries — about how to communicate when your boundaries have been crossed. If letting your true thoughts be known includes making comments that he doesn't appreciate, you need to agree on a way he can tell you that. If he makes cracks about things that are sensitive to you, you need to be able to tell him without getting angry, defensive, or crying.

Just like with a Halloween costume, the mask can be more attractive or more hideous than what's underneath. But I'd rather know — and let him see — the real self, rather than waiting months — or years. Only then, can you make an informed decision whether the true person is someone you want to be with or not.

Are you afraid to speak up for fear of losing him?

I'm amazed at the number of accomplished, assertive, confident midlife women who confide in me a problem with their dating relationship. The common sense solution is to talk to their guy about it.

However, many of these women seem squeamish at this prospect. When I ask why, they respond, "I'm afraid of losing him."

Women don't speak up because they are afraid of losing him

I point out that if a man stops seeing you because you speak up about something that isn't working or is bothersome to you, he shouldn't be in your life anyway. As long as you share your concern in a straightforward, non-judgmental, non-angry way, if he jumps ship he doesn't have the emotional stability or the interest in you to warrant a relationship with you.

The fear comes if you feel he is "perfect" for you and you don't want to jeopardize it. However, when you realize that perfect needs to include "willing to talk things through" or "ability to work things out," and he bails, he isn't perfect.

And maybe he is willing to work it out but you haven't given him the opportunity because of your fear. That isn't fair to either of you.

So if you find yourself withholding issues that can't be ignored, you need to examine your trust in your man's ability to hear your concerns and discuss them maturely and rationally. But by not sharing, you are preventing you both from creating an even better relationship, and short shifting his capacity to maturely discuss issues.

You have done your best to communicate maturely and he responds this way, best to know it now as he doesn't have the skills for a long-term relationship.

You can alleviate some of the tenseness by admitting your concern: "I have something I need to discuss with you but I'm not sure how you'll react. I want to share openly and honestly and for us to have a mature discussion." Then if he reacts otherwise you have all the information you need to move this man out of your life.

What's his inclination to work things out?

Bemoaning to a psychologist friend the tale of a recent particularly jarring breakup, he said, "You need to ask better questions early on." He was right. I thought I was reasonably good about asking important questions, but I hadn't asked the one he suggested.

I painfully learned that my beau of many months had no interest in working out anything that wasn't exactly what one of us wanted. He barely tolerated my bringing up any of my unmet needs and finding a mutually agreeable solution. However, in this breakup I learned that if something wasn't as he wanted it, he just called it quits. No attempt to discuss it or explore a solution. I couldn't imagine how anyone would expect a relationship to be perfect without any modifications, but that apparently was his perspective.

My psychologist friend suggested asking within the first few dates, "What do you tend to do if something in the relationship isn't working for you?" This would tell me if the guy had any interest in bringing it up and discussing it, rather than just calling it quits or going poof.

I don't know how my now ex-beau would have answered if I'd asked the question, as I felt sometimes he said what he thought I wanted to hear. So conceivably he could have said, "We'd discuss it." But since he was a master sweet talker, I can also imagine him saying, "We are a perfect match, so I don't see anything that wouldn't work for me." He was very good at evasiveness, even when I pressed him.

I can understand not wanting to approach working it out if someone is abusive or emotionally unstable. I have had two beaus who I learned were so defensive that I couldn't bring up issues without them flying off the handle. But I made sure I let them know we wouldn't be continuing, even if I didn't say, "…because you are wacko." That would not have been good. So I just said that I was clear we weren't a fit, that I enjoyed the good times we shared, and I wished them the very best. So in these cases, I, like my recent beau, was not willing to work it out. But that was only after some tumultuous attempts that showed me it was an uphill battle.

What have you learned are good questions to ask early in dating someone that shed some light on his philosophy about working out any kinks in a generally good relationship?

The sticky side of honey do's

A past beau called the little chores he did for me around my house "honey dues" and implied they were the dues men paid to make their woman happy.

I've generally thought it was sweet and loving when a man offered or agreed to help with small household jobs that I either couldn't do alone or didn't have the expertise to accomplish. Usually I call a handyman when I need help, but often a beau has offered assistance.

Honey do's can be simple household maintenance acts via which a man shows his caring for you. A man replaced my leaking kitchen sink faucet to one with more features and no drips, for which I am appreciative every day. Another consolidated my audio equipment into a home entertainment center, which I love. Both men are gone from my life, but their thoughtful deeds live on and remind me of their kindnesses.

But sometimes I've paid more dearly to have my man's help than to pay my handyman.

For example, one beau insisted on waxing my car, even though I didn't ask and really didn't care if it was waxed or not. He started late in the day and it was dark by the time it was ready to be wiped off, so he decided to finish it in the morning. By that time it was caked on so hard, some parts never came off. Even after many washings and many months there were still remnants of that wax. It reminded me of him — and his overbearing ways that this represented — every time I looked at it and long after we broke up.

A recent sweetheart offered to install a new rod and curtains in my dining room. I was appreciative of his offer and helped him determine the right length. I was then distracted by a phone call and when I returned I discovered he'd hung them 4 too short. He noticed and offered to rehang them on a future visit, but before he could he broke up with me. So now every time I see them I think of him and have mixed feelings of gratitude for his doing this chore for me and irritation that he hung them poorly. It reminds me of my other requests about the relationship — not honey do's — he feigned to attend to but didn't.

Some acts, like the unwanted wax job, are more a way a man shows what he thinks you should have, not necessarily what you want or need. And while these are ways he shows he cares for you, they may not be ways you want to be cared for.

All in all, it's probably best to just hire a handyman as you'll have fewer upsets, both while in the relationship and after your guy is gone.

When is it too early to say "I love you"?

Adventures in Delicious Dating After 40 reader Mike asks:

> *How long into a relationship is it healthy to say I love you? Is it 2, 3, 6 months? I'm always told I'm doing it too early. I say it when I feel it. However when the relationship ends my women friends tell me I've said it too early. I've also had women tell me they love me before I feel it's appropriate. Is there a time frame I don't know about?*

Dear Mike:

No, there is no time frame. But I do think a month or two is a tad early because you are still in the infatuation stage and really don't know the other person. It takes months to uncover who someone really is, and it can take a lot longer if s/he is good at keeping on a mask or being who they think you want them to be. So you can say, "I adore you" or "I care about you" but the "L" word is so charged, I avoid using it until I really feel it - and it seems the other is feeling it too.

We make those words mean so much, like "I will stand by you and work out any hiccups," "I have no interest in anyone else," or other vows of long-term commitment. However, those three words really mean none of those things. Men have told me they love me, then broken up with me soon thereafter. My ex-husband told me he still loved me after he left me. He wasn't trying to reconcile, just trying to assure me (I think) that his decision wasn't out of hatred of me. It can be confusing to hear the words that we take to mean so much and see actions that don't reinforce our interpretation. That's why it's important to use them sparingly until you are in a solid relationship.

Yesterday a man with whom I've been communicating online and on the phone for a few weeks told me he was in love with me. I thought it was sweet, but I also know until one has met and spent considerable time together, he can only believe he is in love with the person he thinks me to be. But it is highly unlikely he is in love with the real me. I've learned the words can be uttered when you are feeling connectedness, fondness or infatuation, but not true love. You have to know someone to feel that depth of emotion.

I explored other issues around too-soon "I love yous" in "When he tells you he loves you."

What are you pretending not to know?

In dating relationships, it's easy to ignore your guy's disrespectful behaviors or indicators that he isn't for you. You justify it by saying that you like many things about him so you're willing to overlook some less-than-perfect behaviors.

But you're just being an ostrich burying your head in the sand of romance.

In the book The Art of Living Consciously by Nathaniel Branden, the author says to ask yourself, "What am I pretending not to know?" I know I would have ended unsuitable relationships earlier if I'd paused to honestly answer that question. I ignored glaring signs that a man was not for me.

You could pretend not to know:

💜 He's not considerate of you. For example, he calls you when it is convenient to him, not to you. You are not a morning person and he insists on calling you on his way to work — at 6:30!

💜 He doesn't keep his word. He says he'll call you the next day and it is several days before you hear from him.

💜 He's not trustworthy. He says he's not interested in seeing anyone else, but you see he's on the dating site within the last 24 hours.

💜 He's not as into you as he claims. You've been going out at least once a week for 3 months and he says you are the one for him, but you have yet to meet any of his friends or go to his home.

💜 He's miserly. He claims to have lots of investments, good income and no debt yet he only takes you to Chili's, Applebee's and movie matinees.

Or you could pretend not to know something about your own behaviors.

💜 You say you really like him, yet you let his calls go to voice mail as you finish something inconsequential.

You could pretend not to know something about your own behaviors.

💜 You turn down gal pal invitations because he says you might get together. But then he doesn't call. Again.

💜 You carry your cell phone everywhere — even to the bathroom — because he calls unpredictability and you don't want to miss it.

💜 You allow yourself to move more quickly than you're really comfortable. Within weeks he has moved clothes and toiletries into your home asking for an empty drawer. And you let him as you like having someone around even though he has obnoxious behaviors that are inconsiderate and hurtful.

💜 You hear yourself asking him, "When will I see you?" even though you know it sounds needy, but you don't seem to be able to shut your trap.

To make what you're pretending to not know more real, write down the things you notice but decide to ignore. What have you've noticed in the past that you wish you'd taken heed of?

Forfeiting being right for being loving

I recently spent time with a long-married couple. Like nearly all long-term couples, they've developed habits they don't even know they have. One of this couple's favorite ones, it seems, is bickering over inconsequential details. For example, "We went shopping last Thursday…" "No, it was Wednesday." "No, I'm sure it was Thursday." Etc., etc., etc.

It got to the point where I could stand it no longer. I finally blurted out, "It really, really doesn't matter what day it was." That got them to move on.

I decided if they were to argue over one more insignificant thing, I would attempt to help them see what they were doing. I readied my sentence: "You two are forfeiting being loving for being right." I never had to utter it, which I'm not sure is good news. Lucky for me I didn't have to endure more bickering. But I also think my observation might have made them think, if they were willing to hear it.

But whether it would be a lesson for them or not, it was a reminder for me. Early in my marriage I repeated the same pattern I learned from my parents: bickering over idiotic details to prove I was right. They would argue daily over facts that had no consequence. They were each determined to show they were right — even though they sacrificed being loving.

After lots of couples' counseling, I finally saw that my behavior was driving a wedge between my husband and me. It was disrespectful, emasculating, and accomplished nothing productive. I eliminated 90%-95% of this habit. I'll not claim 100% success, as I don't know that I was ever completely cured.

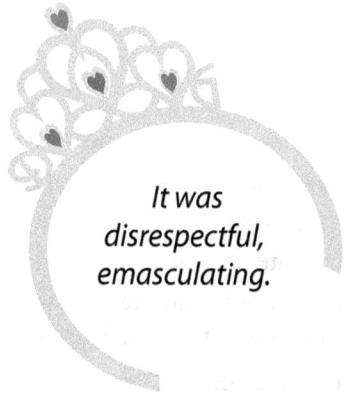

It was disrespectful, emasculating.

When exploring new relationships, it's important to be aware of old behaviors that sabotaged past relationships. If you don't know your irksome behaviors, I'm sure past loves would be happy to share their list! But knowledge is not the Holy Grail — but it is the start. Changing habits is one of the hardest things in life. But if you are motivated to have a loving relationship, you have to be willing to give up non-loving habits — and the need to always be right.

"He can change"

I heard the male version of this the other day from a friend pining for an ex-girlfriend.

Yes, people can change. Some can change at the snap of their fingers, vowing to stop or start a behavior immediately. A few actually accomplish that.

Others change after starts and restarts, taking days/weeks/months/years/decades to adopt the new behavior. Some are eventually successful; others never are.

And some people have no desire to make the change, even though they tell you (and perhaps themselves) they do. They make the verbal commitment and maybe some half-hearted attempts (or not!), but never shift one iota.

But nearly all of us do change. Some consciously and with effort to become better. Some, with no consciousness or effort, allow their bad habits to become worse. Very few midlife people behave exactly the way they were in high school or college.

Some people change out of a self-motivated desire to become a better person. Some change because they know it will make a loved one happier or less annoyed.

And some refuse to change out of spite for someone, knowing a certain behavior sends them up the wall.

The problem with wanting someone to change for you to be happy with them is you will be unhappy until 1) they do, or 2) you accept them the way they are.

There's an old saying that women enter a relationship expecting to change a man and men enter a relationship hoping the woman won't change.

Deciding to stay in a relationship predicated upon the other person changing is asking for heart ache for both parties. You will never be happy unless they make the change. They will not be happy as they know you aren't completely happy with them.

I've entered relationships thinking I can remodel the man into someone who fits my ideal. Have I been able to influence some behavior changes? Sure. But ultimately he resented it, just as I have if a man thinks I should be different than I am and tries to get me to conform to his idea of perfection.

When a 21-year-old relative was complaining about her live-in boyfriend, I asked her, "If he were to be exactly the same in 5 years, would you be happy?" The answer was "no." If you can't live with the man he is now, don't make it permanent. People will change. We can't control that. It's part of being a growing human being. But if you are in the relationship counting on him to change for the better, you should move on.

"*Women are work!*"

He said this with exasperation. He was weary from his last relationship being more effort than he would have liked. He thought it should be easier.

I told him most relationships were are least some work. They could be easy breezy, but there was some "work" involved — one of you had to initiate contact, you had to be willing to work through any hiccups. This could be considered work by some. And when romance is involved, expectations quickly escalate.

I've heard similar laments from others — mostly men. They didn't want a relationship to be work. Which usually means they want to do what they want when they want and not have to be responsible for their sweetie's expectations. Which is what got my friend into his "women are work" funk. His last lady expected him to call her regularly and initiate outings — after dating only two weeks. He then had to deal with her angst when she got upset that he wasn't behaving as she wanted. "Work" indeed.

I believe that a healthy relationship should be minimal "work" yet it needs constant attention. "Work" says that it's above and beyond what you find pleasurable.

You have to do too many things that you'd prefer not to do. Every romantic relationship requires some compromise, some adaptation, some doing what you'd not choose to do on your own.

What's your experience with "work" in a relationship? When is it too much? Too little?

An awkward situation

In midlife dating, we sometimes encounter situations that are just too awkward to have a ready-made answer. I remember one from early in my dating re-entry. I wish I could forget it. I'm not sure I would have an easy answer if it happened again.

The gentleman and I were dating a few months and neither of us were exploring dating others, not because of any overt exclusivity discussion. More because we were busy and not unhappy with the relationship, although I wouldn't say I was happy either. It was a relationship of convenience — at least for me.

We saw each other at least once on the weekend and once during the week. At first he paid for all dinners, and I'd pay for the movie or after-dinner drink or dessert on the way home. Then I stepped up and took turns treating for dinners, too. Although at the time, my divorce had taken a major economic toll on my life. When my ex left, my expenses doubled immediately and my income went down dramatically as I just couldn't market my services with much gusto.

So when it was my turn to treat, I'd suggest a modest restaurant. When it was his turn, he nearly always chose an upscale one, as he liked wine and fancy meals. Not that I mind those, but he was more insistent about them than me.

One day he asked, "Would you like to go to the Peobo Bryson/James Ingram concert?" I like those artists, but not so much that I would drive the hour to see them and pay a high ticket price. But my beau liked me to accompany him to events like this, so I said yes. He made an attempt to buy the tickets online, but couldn't complete the transaction. He called me: "I have a client call in 3 minutes and I can't complete the online transaction. The concert is almost sold out. Can you go online and get the tickets?" What was I to say? I said yes.

The tickets cost more than I would have spent considering my economic situation. I assumed he would pay me back, although he never said he would. When we arrived at the event, he suggested I go to will call while he parked the car. If I did this, I'd miss the opportunity for him to say to the box office, "Can we put this on my credit card?" So I said I'd wait for him at will call while he parked. When he arrived, we asked the clerk for our tickets. Since I'd already paid for them, there was no discussion of payment.

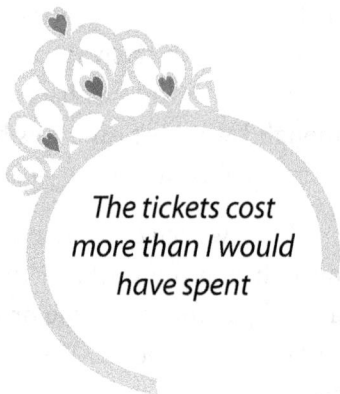

> *The tickets cost more than I would have spent*

I'm a tad embarrassed to share that as I sat through the concert, I couldn't shake dwelling on the high cost of the tickets. And I wasn't enjoying the show that much — probably because I was obsessing about the cost of the tickets.

I felt uncouth and chintzy to bring up the reimbursement for the tickets, so I said nothing. My guy knew I was barely scraping by. How could he not know that this expenditure was more than I'd have volunteered to take on? I stewed and fretted.

It never came up. He was generous to me in some ways, so I justified that I was evening up the score. But I couldn't shake that if I were going to treat for a high-cost event, it would have been for an artist for whom I was a big fan, not just sort of liked. I felt a little duped to treat for an evening I would have never offered to spring for.

This same man had earlier suggested we go to Paris together for vacation. I told him that my finances could not support such a holiday and perhaps we should wait until I could split the costs. He said he understood my situation and would pay for everything if I would use my frequent flyer points to get us business class tickets. So it wasn't as if he didn't know my situation. (We ended up not going because we couldn't get tickets that fit our schedules.)

The tit and tat of finances during dating can be dicey. More so when you are going out together a lot and/ or seeing each other for a while. I now know that this is something that should not be taken for granted but discussed if there is any discomfort.

How do you manage some sense of fairness about dating costs when you've been dating someone for a while?

Your sweetie's and your kids aren't similarly accomplished

Here's a recent question.

There are usually inequalities when you are dating. One person has a more successful career. One person is better at interpersonal skills, and the other is better at technical skills. Differences that makes life interesting and the world go around.

I have accomplished kids. All of them will graduate from college, and have the potential for decent careers. They have their flaws, but are typical middle class, suburban, kids. The kind of kids where you can share their accomplishments when friends are talking about their kids.

I'm getting to know a woman who I think may be someone special. She seems like a decent middle-class person, but has made some bad choices in men — philanderer, alcoholic, etc. However, her kids are a lot less successful than mine. One had a promising military ca-

reer until a genetic predisposition to alcoholism reared its ugly head. The younger two are content to just get by in life. In talking with her about her past relationships, she mentioned wanting the American Dream: husband, house, and kids.

We are both past the having babies stage, but I wonder about the inequality of our families. All the kids are old enough that they won't be living together. But, I just started wondering if the inequality will bread resentment. I can provide a husband and a house. But for kids, we will have to play the cards that have already been dealt.

While I don't have kids, that won't stop me from having an opinion!

If you do become connected with this woman, you can't help but hear about her kids and sharing about yours. At some point, they will meet each other. If she wasn't secure that she did the very best job she could in parenting and admitting that some of how kids turn out is a crap shoot, I imagine she'd feel a bit jealous of your kids' accomplishments.

If she does show any feelings of inadequacy or jealousy and they are unabated, it will ruin the relationship. However, even two parents with accomplished children can have issues about one-up-manship. If you decide to continue seeing her, you have to be conscious about not oversharing about your kids and offering advice about hers. Let this unfold as you build trust and confidence with each other. And wait until she asks you for advice on her offspring.

How spontaneous

are you?

I'm struck that many men's online profiles say they want a spontaneous woman. It's made me look at my own level of spontaneity.

My experience of spontaneity is that someone else (a friend or suitor) calls or shows up and says, "Hey, I'm on my way to XXX. Wanna come?"

More often than not, I have my morning, afternoon, or evening planned so I have to quickly sort my day's priorities and see if I can shift things if I want to accompany them. If I decline, I usually hear disappointment or even chiding from the other.

While I appreciate they wanted to spend some time together, I feel much more special if they take the time to think ahead and invite me the day before. Then I can have time to rearrange my activities and look forward to the outing.

Being invited at the last minute feels like I'm an afterthought. This isn't very appealing.

In fact, I've come to think of these impulsive invitations as selfish. The inviter has had time to decide that the activity is something they want to do and arrange their life to do it. There is no forethought of my schedule or priorities. It is all about them and their desires, and my attendance is not just secondary, but way down the list.

So how does one allow some spur-of-the-moment activities in a planned life? The key is to not be so rigid that you can't occasionally say, "I'll do my projects tomorrow."

And I try to educate my friends and suitors that I do well with planned spontaneity. Although it sounds like an oxymoron, it means that we decide to spend the afternoon, evening, or day together, perhaps float some possible activities, then agree to decide when we're together. This allows for the proper clothing to be worn or brought or other items that would fit with the activities offered.

For example, a friend stayed with me over the weekend to attend a meeting Saturday. She had Sunday to play. Saturday night we discussed a handful of options that encompassed what she wanted to do. Sunday morning we set out on our top priority, then at transition points throughout the day I offered her options. The day unfolded wonderfully as we ebbed and flowed based on the weather, our mood and our hunger. We were spontaneous within a loosely planned day.

Addressing kissing
mismatch

I'm dating someone I'm very attracted to, and we have lots of good chemistry on a variety of levels. The only issue I feel the need to question is the way she kisses.

When I move in to kiss her, she appears to retreat within herself and becomes passively accepting. She barely moves a muscle to kiss me back, so I feel like I'm kissing someone who is asleep. I've tried kissing her all kinds of ways — soft & hard, lips & tongue, dry & wet, shallow & deep, high & low, short & long, and yet she just doesn't reciprocate. She's otherwise a very sensitive and sensual person, and she says that connection and intimacy are important to her. She says she quite likes me and that she's turned on when we kiss.

I had a therapist once who said this kind of behavior could be indicative of some kind of previous sexual abuse, so I wonder if that could be something. We haven't been dating long, so it's entirely possible she hasn't told me of some traumatic experience in her past. Or maybe she's just shy or just doesn't like the way I kiss.

Equal participation and reciprocation is important to me in all areas of a relationship, and I feel that passive kissing is generally a bad sign that a person is not assertive enough to handle their side of the equation. It may be too early to have that discussion with her.

I want to address this before we go much further. I'm able to bring up "difficult" topics, I just don't know how to approach this one. My first guess says be straight-forward and positive, "I enjoy kissing you, and I would love it if you kissed me back." But that sounds kinda blunt.

Another approach is potentially invasive, "I notice that when I kiss you, you seem to freeze up. I'm wondering where you go when that happens and what your thoughts are."

William

How about starting just a tad softer with something like, "I love the sensuality of kissing and get quite turned on when my woman also seems to enjoy it. What's your perspective on kissing?" Then you're inviting her to share. You can even say, "What kind of kissing do you like?"

I've dated men who's kisses didn't turn me on or that actually turned me off. I said to one man overtly, "Let me show you how I like to be kissed." That lasted a little while, but then we stopped seeing each other, but it wasn't only about kissing.

So if you like her and feel it's worth the effort, open the conversation!

DG

Do you bust his ...
chops?

en often show their connection by teasing and good-naturedly insulting each other. They can make pot shots about the other's weight, thinning hair, bulbous nose, incompetencies, shortcomings or lack of sexual prowess without taking it personally.

So what happens when a woman — especially a woman he's attracted to — tries to join in the boys' club teasing?

Not good.

Some women have trouble understanding that many men take it especially hard when a woman busts a man's... chops. So if the woman he's dating joins in the fray when his friends are torquing his jaw, it doesn't feel like chops she's busting to him; it feels like she's attacked his sensitive man parts.

It took me a long time to learn this. I can quickly join in the busting repartee. All my life I have found myself the only woman in a group of male friends or colleagues so picked up the behaviors they have among the guys.

The problem is, men don't take teasing from a woman as they would from a man. Decades ago a gal pal pulled me aside and told me to not teasingly put down my then-husband. It took me a while as he laughed when I teased him. But I did reduce and eventually stop this behavior with him, as I began to see it was not the right dynamic for us.

A year ago, a male friend asked me to "be nice" to him in front of his girlfriend. When I sincerely said, "You mean I'm not always nice to you?" He said no, sometimes I zinged him in front of her. I apologized and realized he was right. I vowed to build him up in front of her, not tear him down. I eliminated my zingers, whether she was around or not. And I promised myself I'd stop myself from the temptation to do that to any man.

So why do women zing men?

It can elicit laughter, often from the target himself.

It makes her feel like she's accepted by the guys.

She feels special because other women aren't given such alpha status.

She doesn't think it hurts the target.

She has low self-esteem so it makes her feel good to put down others.

Most men would not let on that it was uncomfortable — or downright hurtful — to receive zingers from a woman, especially a woman with whom he was involved. They may laugh it off, but it can hurt and he'll never let on. So the women think they are just playing around, that the guys like it or it doesn't affect them.

Have you zinged men? If so, why? Did you learn to stop?

Love advice from a Frenchman

Over a pain au chocolat in Paris, my French friend Benoit shared relationship advice. While it was something I'd heard before, somehow coming from a French man in Paris, delivered in his charming French accent, it had more gravitas.

DG: Benoit, the French have an international reputation for love, romance and sensuality. You've been married over two decades. What do you attribute your long-term relationship success to?

Benoit: It ez very zimple. Anyone can understand.

DG: OK. Tell me.

Benoit: You must court your love az long az you are together.

DG: Is that it? Is there more?

Benoit: I tell my wiv I love her every day. I tell her in different wayz.

DG: Like what?

Benoit: One day I tell her she is beautiful. Another day I tell her I love how she smellz. Another, how sexy she is. Another, what a good cook she iz. I compliment her on the different thingz I love about her.

DG: Does she do the same?

Benoit: She tellz me in different wayz. I know she lovez me.

DG: And you feel that is the secret to your long-term happiness?

Benoit: Abzolutely! We appreciate each other every day.

So there you have it — straight from a Frenchman's lips! I agree with him wholeheartedly. Dating and courting never end. It keeps the allure and passion alive.

Now, if I could just find a Frenchman with whom to try out this idea.

Resources

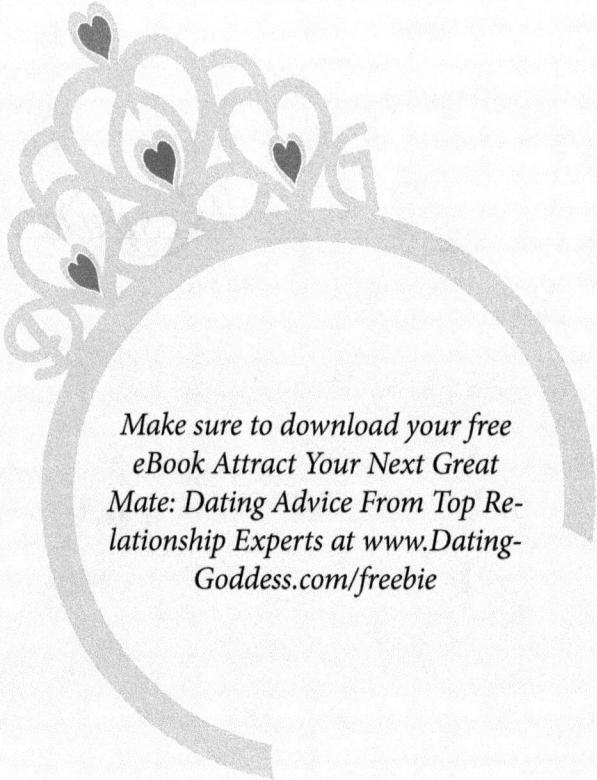

Make sure to download your free eBook Attract Your Next Great Mate: Dating Advice From Top Relationship Experts at www.Dating-Goddess.com/freebie

Afterword

At the time of this writing, I have not yet found my true King Charming. I continue my search with verve. I've become more discerning about what I want and don't want. I've met some wonderful men pals — my treasures — who continue to be in touch.

I wish you much luck in your adventure. It will be fun and frustrating, exhilarating and exasperating, and sexy or sexless. So much depends on you, your approach and your attitude. My books are designed to help you enjoy as much as possible and ward off unpleasantness. But nearly all adventures have wonderful highs as well as a few lows. If you know that going in and arm yourself with information on what to expect, you'll have more of the positives and fewer of the negatives.

Please drop by www.DatingGoddess.com and join in the discussion and report on your experiences.

Dating Goddess

Resources

Go to www.datinggoddess.com to access a variety of useful resources. We work to suggest resources we think have value.

Dating and relationship book reviews

These reviews will save you time and money as I've given you my take on specific books, CDs and more. Some are worth your effort to buy and read or listen to them — some are not. We're always adding new book reviews, so check frequently. We'll also notify our mailing list when new resources are added.

Dating site links

There are a lot of dating sites on the Internet. I've listed the ones I think are worth investigating.

Dating products and tools

Dating can be daunting. We're continually looking at

ways to make it easier and more fun. We'll provide info on games, tools, even date-wear that will help others know you're available, or help you get to know potential suitors better.

Dating and relationship advice sites

Advice "experts" abound on the Internet as anyone can self-proclaim themseves as expert — even if they haven't dated in 30 years and never in midlife. I've worked to find experts who's advice I generally think is solid.

Midlife recources

We'll feature Web sites, books, events and other resources we think might interest you.

Newly discovered resources

I'll add other resources as we discover them, subscribe to our mailing list to get the scoop as soon as we find them. Go to www.DatingGoddess.com to register for our mailing list. Don't worry, we won't sell or give your email to anyone.

Acknowledgments

Let me start by acknowledging the 112 men who helped trigger the lessons contained in this book. Some prompted several! They remain nameless here to protect their identity, although most would recognize references to them. Plus the thousands more whose winks, emails and calls didn't result in a date, but helped me learn the dating game. And all those men who I emailed who never responded — such a blessing to have them weed themselves out.

I acknowledge the 112 men who triggered my lessons

I'd like to thank my Seven Sisters mastermind group for the tremendous brainstorming, noodling, strategizing and encouragement. I wouldn't have begun this project without the prodding of Val Cade, Chris Clarke-Epstein, Mariah Burton Nelson, Sue Dyer, Sam Horn and Marilynn Mobley.

Thank you to my good friends who've listened to my dating stories ad nauseam, and whose support and wisdom are embedded in this text. Ed Betts, Ken Braly, Bruce Daley, Tom Drews, Elaine Floyd, Paulette Ensign, Scott Friedman, Craig Harrison, Mary Jansen, Tom Johnson, Sandy Jones, Mary Kilkenny, Ellie Klevins, Patrick Lynch, Mary Marcdante, Barbara McNichol, Ann Peterson, Anthony Ramsey, Caterina Rando, Kristy Rogers, Jana Stanfield, Holly Steil, Terry Tepliz, and George Walther, thank you.

The Adventures in Delicious Dating After 40 series

The *Adventures in Delicious Dating After 40* series is designed to help you understand your own midlife dating journey. It is not a road map, as we all take different routes. It is a guide to help you understand yourself, midlife men, and the dating process. Hopefully, you'll not only learn from the lessons and insights shared in this series, but you'll examine how they apply — or don't — to your own dating adventure.

You'll get the scoop on what you need to know, what's changed since you last dated, and how to navigate inevitable bumps in the road.

Following is an overview of each book in the series and a sampling of some of the chapter titles. All are detailed at www.DatingGoddess.com.

Date or Wait: Are You Ready for Mr. Great?

Are you ready for a special man in your life? You have a great life. But you know you'd like a special man to share it. You think you're ready to date, but you haven't done it in a while.

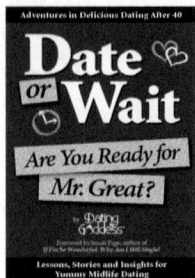

What should you consider before you actually start dating full bore? Even if you've reentered the dating world, this will give you a foundation of attitude and philosophy to make your adventure more fulfilling.

Sample chapters

💜 From hurt to flirt

💜 Dating is like Baskin-Robbins

💜 You've got to kiss a lot of…princes!

💜 What's your definition of dating success?

💜 Are you open to receiving?

💜 Dating: A self-designed personal-growth workshop

💜 Hands-on dating research

💜 Being present to the presents

💜 Being aggressively single

💜 Approaching dating like a buffet

💜 Is Brad Pitt ruining your love life?

💜 Treasures can come in dented packages

Assessing Your Assets: Why You're A Great Catch

You have many wonderful qualities. But it's easy to focus on one's flaws — at least what seem like flaws to you. However, to the right man your imperfections are endearing, attractive and lovable. You have to be clear what you offer a man who will find you enchanting.

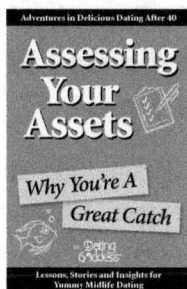

Assessing Your Assets helps you look at what you bring to a new relationship. It will help you see your good points so you'll approach dating with more confidence.

Sample chapters

💜 Don't think you are damaged goods

💜 You are (probably) more attractive than you think!

💜 They aren't called "hate handles"

💜 Are you a good man picker?

💜 What are your deal breakers?

💜 Are you arguing your limitations?

💜 Turn your liabilities into assets

💜 The strong vs. nice woman debate

💜 Is your sense of humor stunting your dating?

💜 Why are we drawn to bad boys?

💜 The zest test

In Search of King Charming: Who Do I Want to Share My Throne?

You are no longer looking for "Prince" Charming because you are a queen. You want someone who is at your level, not groveling at your feet. You want a king — someone who's your equal and with whom you can rule the throne together!

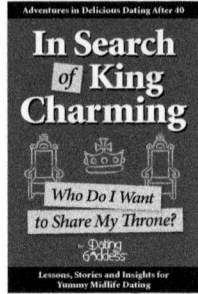

This book focuses on helping you better define what you want beyond tall, dark and handsome! You'll consider characteristics you might not have thought of before. You'll look at what you want now.

Sample chapters

- Building your Franken-boyfriend

- What's your "perfect boyfriend's" job description?

- A man to go with your wardrobe

- In search of the elusive good kisser

- When you're clear on what you want, it appears

- Are you dating the same guy in different bodies?

- Does he fit in your world?

- What's your kissing quotient?

- Is your guy's loving muscle strong?

- Do you both have the same dating rhythm?

Embracing Midlife Men:
Insights Into Curious Behaviors

Do you sometimes scratch your head after interacting with a midlife man, wondering, "What could he possibly be thinking?" Especially if it's before, during or after a date with a man who presumably wants to impress you!

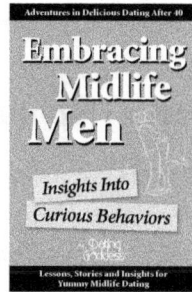

This book focuses on better understanding midlife men's behaviors. When you grasp what's going on in his head it's much easier to embrace him. Men are wondrous creatures, so we need to understand them better and love them for who they are.

Sample chapters

💜 Men are like shoes

💜 Why men disappear when it gets serious

💜 Chivalry isn't dead —but it seems to be hibernating

💜 Do men want feisty women?

💜 Midlife men have forgotten how to date

💜 Are you getting prime time from your man?

💜 When a man tells you what he paid for things

💜 Does he treat you like his ex?

💜 Has Greg Behrendt done women a disservice?

💜 Tales of woo

Dipping Your Toe in the Dating Pool: Dive In Without Belly Flopping

You've decided you are ready — you want to start dating. Maybe you've already had a few coffee dates with several men. You want to be as successful as possible on your dating adventure.

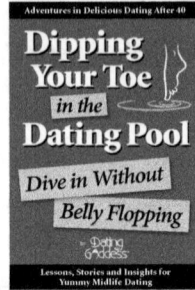

This book focuses on getting started on your dating adventures. We cover what you need to know as you begin your journey.

Sample chapters

- Do you have the right datewear?
- Dating with integrity
- Building your rejection muscle
- When "be yourself" is questionable advice
- Faux beaus and practice dating
- Are you making bad decisions out of loneliness?
- Being "in wonder" about your date's behavior
- When do you feel most vulnerable in dating?
- Are you out of his league — or he yours?
- Why listening is so seductive

Winning at the Online Dating Game: Stack the Deck in Your Favor

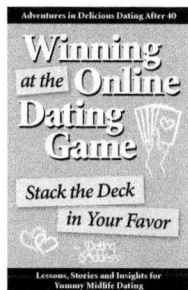

Internet dating can be frustrating or fruitful. It will be much less exasperating if you know how to read and weed out men's profiles that aren't appropriate for you. And you'll have a steady stream of potential suitors if you know how to write a compelling profile for yourself.

This book focuses on the ins and outs of online dating. How to play the game, which has it's own rules and language. If you don't understand how online dating works, you'll waste a lot of time connecting with men who are not a possible fit for you.

Sample chapters

💜 Shopping for men

💜 Safe online dating

💜 Is 21st Century dating unnatural?

💜 What do men look at in your profile?

💜 Euphemisms uncovered

💜 Are you describing yourself compellingly?

💜 No, I will not be dating your Harley

💜 Playing the online dating game

💜 Scantily clothed pictures

Check Him Out Before Going Out: Avoiding Dud Dates

Under the cloak of the anonymity that email and the phone provides, men often reveal more than they intend. If you ask the right questions you can find out a lot about his values and view of the world after just an interaction or two.

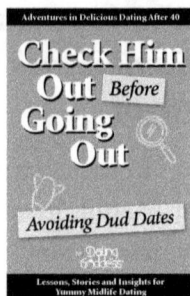

This book focuses on what you need to ask before agreeing to even a coffee date. You need to vet the men who email and call you to ensure you're not likely to waste your time with men who clearly aren't a match.

Sample chapters

❤ Becoming smitten with the fantasy

❤ Can Google help — or hinder — your dating life?

❤ Qualify your potential dates before meeting

❤ The art of consideration

❤ Anticipating a big date is like awaiting Santa

❤ Being seduced by what he is over who he is

❤ Are you his spare?

❤ My boyfriend, whom I haven't met

❤ When canceling is the right thing to do

❤ Politics, religion and sex — oh my!

First-Rate First Dates: Increasing the Chances of a Second Date

You can tell a lot about someone within the first 30 minutes. What does he talk about? Does he ask you questions? If so, what does he want to know about you? What do you need to know about him? How does he treat you? How does he treat those around you?

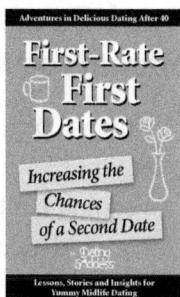

This book focuses on what goes on during the first date. How do you determine if you want a second date? What you can do to increase the likelihood your date will ask you for a second? That is if you want a repeat!

Sample chapters

♥ Start with coffee

♥ How do you greet him?

♥ When it clicks, throw out some of your criteria

♥ Tracking your date's score

♥ Clues a guy is just looking for a booty call

♥ 12 signs he won't be asking for a second date

♥ First-date red flags that this guy isn't for you

♥ Honesty is not always the best policy

♥ Chemistry, or does he make my toes curl?

♥ Women's first-date blunders

Real Deal or Faux Beau: Should You Keep Seeing Him?

You've begun to go out with a man you like. How do you decide if you should continue seeing him, or if you should release him because he's not The One?

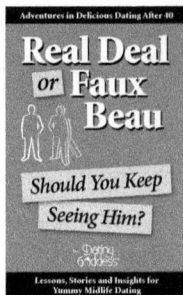

This book focuses on second dates and beyond. During the dating process you are both assessing if you want to keep seeing each other. This book helps you determine what questions you need to ask yourself.

Sample chapters

💜 Deciding to see him again or not

💜 What's your date's Delight/Disappointment Scale score?

💜 Broaching tough conversations

💜 "I want to respect me in the morning"

💜 Does he invite you to his place?

💜 Are you stingy in dating?

💜 When his hand is on your knee too soon

💜 Easy way to ask hard questions

💜 Rose-colored glasses obscure red flags

💜 If his stories don't add up, subtract yourself

Multidating Responsibly: Play the Field Without Being A Player

Playing the field is frowned on in some circles. There are definitely appropriate and inappropriate ways to date several men simultaneously.

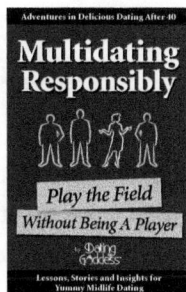

This book focuses on how to date around responsibly and with integrity without leading men on. If you do it with honesty, you can date several people at once until you're both ready to focus only on each other.

Sample chapters

- "Pimpin'" — Dating multiple guys
- Multi-dating pros and cons
- Your Date-A-Base — tracking multiple suitors
- "Hot bunking" your beaus
- Are you a "Let's Make a Deal" type of dater?
- Assume there are other women
- Dating's revolving door
- How long do you hedge your bet?
- Beware of multi-tasking when multi-dating
- Back burner beaus
- The boyfriend phone

Moving On Gracefully: Break Up Without Heartache

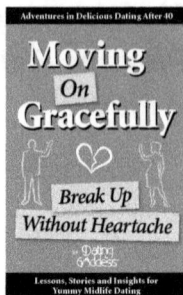

"Breaking up" sounds so high school, doesn't it? But part of the dating process is saying something when one of you decides not to date the other anymore. Going "poof" is not a mature or respectful option in midlife.

This book focuses on surviving a breakup, whether you initiate it or not. Either way, it's never easy to break up if you have developed any fondness toward the other.

Sample chapters

💚 Hello — goodbye: How to say no thanks after meeting

💚 Releasing back into the dating pool

💚 50 ways to leave your lover? 4 ways not to leave your suitor

💚 Breaking up is hard to do — right

💚 Why men go "poof"

💚 How to trump being dumped

💚 When breaking up is a "Get Out of Jail Free" card

💚 How to detect the end is near

💚 Failed relationships' blessings

💚 He's broken up with you — he just didn't tell you

💚 Rejection is protection

From Fear to Frolic: Get Naked Without Getting Embarrassed

This book focuses on what you need to consider and know before getting physically intimate with a man you're dating. This is nerve-wracking to many midlife women. This book will prepare you.

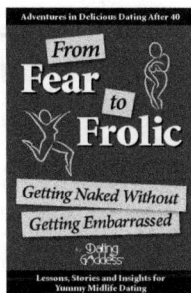

Sample chapters

💜 Sleepover do's and don'ts

💜 Does he want in your life — or just in your bedroom?

💜 Getting naked with him the first time

💜 An excuse to seduce or how important is bedroom bliss?

💜 What to ask yourself before getting naked with him

💜 Are you and your guy on the same sexual time line?

💜 Sharing your sexual owner's manual with him

💜 What women need from a man before having sex

💜 Why too-soon midlife sex is like non-fat food

💜 How dating sex is like waffles

💜 Too-soon seduction: "I'm special, but not THAT special"

Ironing Out Dating Wrinkles: **Work Through Challenges** *Without Getting Steamed*

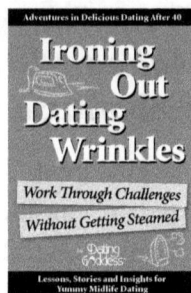

Nearly all relationships have some ups and downs. Part of getting to know someone is knowing how they work through relationship misunderstandings.

This book focuses on how to work through the inevitable hiccups that happen when you are getting to know each other. If you can both deal with challenges, the bond deepens and you find yourself smitten.

Sample chapters

💚 When your guy vexes you, ask what your highest self would do

💚 The first fight

💚 You want boo; he wants boo-ty

💚 Where's the line between getting your needs met and being selfish?

💚 Expressing your upset with your guy

💚 Is his toothbrush in your cabinet too soon?

💚 Do you love how he loves you?

💚 Is he collecting data on how to make you happy?

💚 Be careful of being smitten

💚 Exclusivity: How and when to broach it